A Year
in the Life
a City Commune

LIVING
TOGETHER

MIKE WEISS

Living Together: A Year in the Life of a City Commune

by Mike Weiss

Published by Mike Weiss
Text copyright 1974, 2013 by Mike Weiss
Second edition. Publication date February 6, 2013
ISBN: 978-1461060710

To Berne
for the sustenance
and the laughter

I'm grateful for the help I received from Ross V. Speck, who suggested that I write this book; from Joyce Johnson, whose advice has been sensitive and perceptive; and from my friends, companions, and loved ones—Steve Schultz, Ron Hess, Arlene and Bob Ross, Gale Grumbles, Rick Spaid, and Josh Weiss.

Prologue

My wife Ruth fantasized that her mother and mine would read this book in a dimly lit closet, huddled together to cushion the shock of whatever craziness they might find in it. Sex for instance. What if, in my own perverse way, I were to reveal to the world the most unimaginable configurations of our communal sex life? You see, mine is a family which seldom talks about sex, except to joke, and usually that reticence is fine with me. Once in a while it takes a beating, however. Most recently there was the surprise party for my mother's fiftieth birthday. Friends and relatives had gathered and feasted under the chandelier in my mother-in-law's dining room, and I was secure in the bosom of family conviviality as I relaxed over coffee and dessert. My godmother was asking me about the commune where I live, and I was aware that our conversation was being overheard.

"It's funny," I said a bit louder and more ingenuously than necessary, "how people who don't live in communes always want to know about our sex lives first thing, but at home there's very little talk about sex. We're really just about as uptight as most people, I'd imagine."

"People ask me about your sex life in the house," said my mother, who was sitting nearby.

"What do you think goes on?" my godmother asked her.

"Well," my mother said–and her voice tinkled the way it does when she's anxious but determined–"well, I *assume* Mike and Ruth sleep together, Gary and Anne sleep together, Dan and Leigh sleep together, and Chris and Pete..."

"Sleep together, too," I suggested.

By now everybody was listening: parents, grandparents, cousins, friends. And why not? It was like reading the juiciest part of the book first. And since both Ruth and Anne were pregnant at the time, my family had an understandable interest in just who might be the father of their expected kin.

"I hope the baby looks like Mike." said Ruth's father. A wave of nervous laughter swept along the linen-covered dining table.

"Which baby?" I asked. Some people were laughing so hard that tears were streaming down their cheeks.

Gary, who is Anne's husband, said to my mother, "Well, if you want to know, just ask." In the silence which followed somebody cackled. Just ask, right?

"Have you ever slept with my son Mike?" my mother just asked, turning toward Anne.

Anne couldn't stop laughing long enough to answer the question. When it quieted down a bit, she said in her firm, exclamatory way, "That's the first thing my mother wanted to know. Whether they do it in communes. But she'd never ask me what I did."

A long, one might say, pregnant, pause descended on us until Ruth's mother finally said, "There's still a question on the table."

These mothers were relentless.

"No, I haven't," Anne said.

"I haven't either," Gary roared from beneath his mustache.

"I have," Ruth said softly, and she raised her hand.

Origins

On July 18, 1971, I moved into a big old stone house in the Germantown section of Philadelphia which I shared with eight other people. The twin dogwoods that stood like gatekeepers in our patchy front yard were green and leafy in the summer heat. Now, fourteen months later, as I sit here looking out my bedroom window, the dogwood leaves are thinning and turning rust-red; bright orange-red berries have appeared on the trees, and the days are turning cool again. Seven of us remain in the house, beginning a second year.

Somehow our commune never got a name, although we toyed around with a lot of possibilities in the weeks before and after we moved into the house on Cliveden street. We would sit in a big group on a lawn or in a living room and somebody would say, "How about 'Radish'? It's red and it grows." And two of us would be enthusiastic, three indifferent, and a couple more opposed. We went on like that until we tired of the game and our friends began to call us Cliveden House because it was convenient to call us something, and that name was obvious. I supposed being unable to agree on a name was one of our first lessons in the frustrations of living communally. Our bank, which was unaccustomed to communal accounts with eight co-signers, had the same problem: they finally decided that we were a club, the Cliveden House Club.

Our life together isn't some kind of counter-culture pablum: you do your thing and I'll do my thing and it'll be groovy. We proceed by arrangement. The people in the house didn't just flow into a commune on the tide of life, free and unencumbered. All of us decided to live together individually and in our own separate fashions; we each arrived on Cliveden Street with our own hopes, terrors, needs, fantasies, and ways of getting what we wanted. Gary, for instance, would never have moved in at all if he hadn't planned to leave Philadelphia in a year. He viewed communal living as an experiment, an adventure, and he still does, though as time goes on he finds himself more uncertain about how he will live in the future than he had anticipated. Leigh, on the other hand, was aiming to develop a community where she could bring up the kids she didn't yet have. She's still looking for a lifelong home, but is more hesitant now that she understands better what the cost will be.

Perhaps it was because we recognized from the beginning the many differences in our temperaments, ages, upbringings, beliefs, lifestyles, and desires that our group developed a studied, self-aware style. We work hard at living together, take pride in the happiness of our home, and cause some of our friends to suggest that we are more-communal-than-thou.

I should make it clear at the outset that this is my book. I'm writing it alone at the typewriter in my room On the second floor of the house on Cliveden street. When other people speak–as they will frequently–they say only what I want to set down. Many times I will write about what somebody in the house was thinking or feeling and wherever I do I'm basing my speculation on what the person subsequently told me about what he or she was experiencing at a particular moment, as well as on my increasingly intimate knowledge of the people with whom I live. They have all cooperated with me by spending many hours over many months recalling our life during our first year. Again and again I've been impressed by their candor, and by how well they know one another. Many of my opinions about life in the house were formed listening to and thinking about theirs.

Once in a while, to make the book more true to the spirit of events, I've changed a setting, or altered a sequence. But all the action beginning with Chapter Two occurred between when we first met as a group in the spring of 1971, and July, 1972–our first year.

What you're beginning to read is by no means a collective autobiography. It's my self-centered and self-conscious version of our life together during our first year. So here is my story first: know the source of your information and make your judgements accordingly is my advice.

* * *

I was born about 6 A.M. on October 18, 1942, in Washington, D. C. Soon my father was sent to New Guinea as an Army radio operator, and my mother and I lived most of my first three years with her parents on the Upper West Side of Manhattan. One morning I remember that a man ran into the alley behind the building shouting, "The war is over, the war is over," and not long after that my father appeared at the front door with a blackboard and a rocking horse. He Was pretty much a stranger. My father returned to school and got an accounting degree, and he impressed upon me that being your own boss was the only fundamental freedom. When I was ten years old and my brother was four the family moved to Clearview Gardens, a private development in Whitestone, Queens, where all the 1800 red-brick garden apartments were occupied by Jewish families. Within a year I was part of a tight circle of friends and a larger crowd which went to school together and hung out afterward. We boys played basketball, stickball and touch football year round. School was dreadful, confining and boring, and my street culture fueled my imagination.

Soon we discovered girls. At night, under the street lamps, we flirted, gossiped, giggled, smirked, paired off, broke off, and showed off. I began to get a sense of myself separate from my parents. My identity, such as it was, was derived primarily through my tightness with my friends–I fantasized a utopian community in which we would all live in wealth and comfort, commuting by helicopter to our jobs in the city. And I had developed a case of galloping grumpy adolescence by the time I met Ruth, who, like me, was working for our high school newspaper. She listened sympathetically, and I fell in love while we still wore braces.

By the time I went to Knox College in Galesburg, Illinois, I thought of myself as an outsider, and was convinced that they–everybody in authority and everybody who complied with authority–were full of shit. But I also wanted to belong, I didn't want to be lonely.

Looking back, I can see the beginning of the communal desire in that unfocused, inexperienced wish to belong without belonging to the Big Lie. Over the years that sense of moral necessity has worked itself out as a desire to build a reasonable, happy, peopled life shaped, as much as possible, by my convictions. I read Paul Goodman's book Growing Up Absurd, and it was a revelation of possibilities, and so I read more of his work. From him I learned to give serious consideration to implausible ideas so long as they were sensible; he gave me a respect for the seriousness of the unlikely. For a brash, outspoken and uncomfortable New Yorker living through four years in an unfamiliar, Christian, corn-filled world where girls called other girls guys, that was quite a sanction and quite a confirmation. And to my father's instruction to be my own boss Goodman added the idea of meaningful work, gave me a feeling for the interplay of vocation and values–a sense of how they shaped each other and the person.

Ruth and I went through a long, erratic romance and finally decided to get married soon after we both graduated. Instead, she became pregnant one passionate night in the Hotel Custer and we were married at sundown by a pig-farming justice of the peace who agreed to keep Jesus out of the ceremony. She dropped out of school and we lived on the second floor of a gray clapboard house where our son Matthew was born on the last day of 1963.

The next year I went to graduate school in the Writing Seminars at The Johns Hopkins University in Baltimore, Maryland. Ruth was working in a department store to support us, and we were cramped and unhappy. Neither of us had learned to express ourselves emotionally except that I could rant and she could cry. I was absorbed in being a graduate student/writer, and Ruth was going bats about her lack of fulfillment and satisfaction. We crippled through that year and the next, and always put a good face on our marriage in public, where I was a Regular Guy and She was Sensitive.

In the summer of 1966 I went to work for the *Baltimore News-American*, a Hearst newspaper. When my boss bawled at me across the city room, "Hey, kid, c'mere," I dashed up to his desk feeling that I had it made: I was a news Paper reporter–a role whose romantic mingling of cynicism, cronyism, and idealism suited me fine. After awhile I joined the Baltimore Evening Sun, the prestige competition, where I fit in much better: I had that college-punk-button-down-supercilious-good-government-cordovan-shoe image. I covered the state government and felt like I was just beginning to hit my stride. Ruth and I separated and she went back to college; when we decided to live together again she was more confident of herself, I was more certain of what I wanted and felt less like I had been trapped, and our marriage seemed pleasant and friendly. About a year later when I was shatteringly hurt by my oldest, closest friend, Ruth helped me to examine the pieces one at a time. After that, it was easier to risk other losses: I learned that there were unexpected frontiers inside of me, a lesson which eased my way toward a communal future. For the first time I wanted to talk about my fears about myself, my hopes, my doubts. For three or four months Ruth and I talked non-stop about ourselves to each other. I think that was the first time I listened respectfully to what she had to say about herself.

Smoking dope had become a part of our lives. It loosened us up and made our talking and loving and eating more expressive and less inhibited. But more than that: using drugs made me feel I was in a secret tribe outside the limits. By day I was Clark Kent, by night Super-Head. I was the first reporter in Baltimore to wear bellbottoms at work and to let his hair grow over his ears. Thinking back, they seemed like such pathetic gestures, but at the time I had to assert my sense of difference and disenchantment somehow, and I knew no better way. Around the same time I read Skinner's book Walden Two and reacted like a freak in an R. Crumb cartoon trucking on down the street with an exclamation point in his thought cloud. I attached myself to the *Walden* Two vision of community. But, meanwhile, back on the job. . . .

. . . I was covering the Maryland legislature, Governor Spiro Agnew, and the state bureaucracy. My personal urgency and excitement made my work seem boring for the first time, and even though I was superficially successful, I began to feel like a failure and to be hamstrung by the limitations of daily journalism. Politically, I was losing faith in our government's capacity to shape the good life, because I had met few people in City Hall or the State House who had any conception of what they were after beyond getting a job done. I flew around the country with Agnew when he ran for Vice-President in 1968, and was again frustrated by my inability to convey what a danger he was, the dread I felt in the presence of his supporters, how he self-righteously pandered to the fright of decent people who were bathed by the complications of the world. Agnew lacked an imagination, and nobody is more dangerous than an unimaginative pedant with a lust for power. The last campaign piece I wrote was a long analysis of his campaign which ran one edition before being killed by my managing editor. who called it vicious, biased journalism. I didn't even try to explain to him how hard I had tried to maintain an objectivity in which I no longer had any faith. I had become alienated from the source of my income, and so, not long after, I quit, and Ruth, Matthew, and I left Baltimore in search of our future.

I was bitter and I was hurt and I wanted to remake the world, a mighty ambition. Beginning in December, 1969. Ruth and Matthew and I lived in a house my parents owned in the Catskill Mountains. The snow fell four feet deep and at evening we would sit and watch the sun turn the sky purple and orange across the frozen lake. For months I didn't read a newspaper, after years of reading four and me a day. I cut our firewood and got a taste of what it really meant to live away from city bustle; meanwhile our savings were running out, our panic was mounting, and our resolve stiffening. Ruth began to look for a job and when she found one that she wanted as a staff worker for the Medical Committee for Human Rights, we moved to Philadelphia, and began to learn how to live on very little money. Ruth was just starting to take an interest in the women's movement, and through her work we met and became friendly with people who were calling themselves communists or socialists or revolutionaries. That was mind-blowing for me, because covering traditional politics I had identified myself with the values of that milieu and consequently viewed leftists as some kind of fringe lunatics-hard-eyed, humorless conspirators. I found, though, that I liked a lot of Ruth's new friends, that we agreed a lot, and that I could have fun with them. Ruth suggested that I should share the cooking and dishwashing equally with her, and I adapted easily to that change.

Discovering the left, and then finding myself to be part of it, was all I needed to ready myself for a commune. Reading about Cuba and China, learning something about the alternatives to capitalism, gave me a political perspective on my dissatisfactions. And the Movement gave me that important sense of belonging which I had lacked as a reporter. Politically and philosophically, I threw myself into collectivity. I was ripe for the plucking, and two new friends, Gil and Wendy, asked us if we wanted to join with them to form a commune. Faced with a proposition more immediate than my Utopian fantasies, I was frightened: what if they wanted to share sex? would they see that under my disguises I was shallow and uncommitted? would the hidden, hurtful realms of our marriage be revealed? Ruth wanted to take up their offer; she liked them, and she thought that if we shared expenses we could live in a place that wasn't as crummy as what we could afford on our own. I don't know what decided me in the end. I had persuaded myself that socialistic sharing and emotional honesty and openness were desirable, and even though my new beliefs were both abstract and voguish I wanted to act on them. It turned out to be the right thing for me to do.

9

The five of us lived for a year in a house we also shared for several months with one other friend and with Ruth's brother D. R., who dropped out of college and stayed with us for a while. I didn't feel out of place, in fact I was right at living with other people. My decision to live in a commune seemed to how from my sense of myself as an outsider, from my Utopian dreams: from my left-wing politics. I was suited for communal living. Not everybody is, and there's no reason why anybody else should be.

During that year I helped to organize and operate a food co-op in a community close by the University of Pennsylvania called Powelton Village. Each Thursday morning at four I drove a truck to the wholesale produce market where we purchased bushel-basketsful of red apples; cartons wet and stuffed with spinach, lettuce and cabbage; fifty-pound burlap sacks of potatoes and onions; zucchini, peppers. squash, tangerines, oranges, grapefruits, tomatoes. carrots, bananas. I ran around in the dark and cold with a clipboard and a pocket crammed full of cash and receipts, and by the time the sun was appearing over the hazy city we had the truck loaded with food for a thousand people and were heading home to the warehouse where the produce was laid out for purchase.

During that year and on into my first year on Cliveden street I was intellectually committed to a style of living which only partially fulfilled me. I wanted to work only collectively, I was anti-money, I was sometimes strident and rhetorical, I craved the courage for street action, I analyzed all events through the prism of my radicalism. But I was neglecting a part of myself: the person who wrote, who was solitary, who enjoyed no part of himself so much as the rebel against *whatever* ideas and modes prevailed. I took a great pride in that food co-op, in participating in the Mayday demonstration in Washington, in being an active, full-time worker for social and political change. For a year or two that was sufficient–but in the long run it wasn't enough by itself. I had to find better ways of joining my individuality to my yearning for collectivity, my politics with my psychological imperatives. I slowly came to feel unsettled, I had no vocation which spoke to me of a productive future; I was growing uneasy about living off Ruth's income, and she was getting tired of my reliance on her. But I wanted to go on living in a group, and so did Ruth.

Gil and Wendy were planning to leave the commune to travel in Asia and Africa, and we began to think about forming a new household that would last longer than one year. We had been pulling up roots and changing jobs or homes what felt like every few months, and for Matthew's sake as well as our own, we wanted to settle down for awhile.

Ruth had met Dan and Leigh because they were all involved with the politics of health care; Dan was a dropout from his last year of medical school, and Leigh was organizing Health Information Project. They shared a room in a shambles of a house in West Philadelphia where about a dozen people lived, many of them students who seemed to be popping in and out all the time. The place had little feeling of home or warmth or mutuality. Dan and Leigh talked a lot about wanting to live with a tight-knit group.

Our four-way friendship was pleasant, but it didn't give rise to an unusual rapport. Dan and I fantasized a lot about revolutionary adventures. Leigh was put off by those conversations: that dreamy, war-like aspect of Dan made her unsure of herself and impatient with him, and she disliked the way I seemed to bring it out. I was somewhat intimidated by her reputation as a women's movement politico, but I liked her. She had a lovely, friendly smile. And I sensed that she was substantial, I had an immediate confidence that I could rely on her, that what she was and what she.seemed to be were very close to the same. Both she and Dan were mysterious from time to time about some of their political activities. and their secrecy was alluring.

We seemed compatible. Almost nonchalantly one night when they were over for dinner I mentioned that we were interested in the possibility of living together.

"We've been thinking that would be nice, too," Leigh said, and just that simply we decided to form a house. I think we were relieved to have found each other.

Chris was the next to join the group. He was living in the same house that Dan and Leigh were, and they wanted to stay together, which led me to make the mistaken assumption that they were close. Chris and I worked together in the food co-op, and he seemed to have a gentle disposition and a reasonable, conciliatory approach to problems. But he also seemed somewhat helter-skelter, and I wasn't really relaxed around him. When I found out that he was a homosexual I thought that might explain my stiffness with him. I was impressed to learn that he was gay, and thought that living with him would be an opportunity for some new self-exploration. In retrospect I can see how unfair that's been to Chris, treating him as if his sexuality were an experimental problem of some interest to me.

Ruth was charmed by Chris. He modestly accommodated himself to other people's wishes and conceptions, and was likely to remember your birthday, your favorite foods, and your mother's maiden name before you were even sure of who he was. It wasn't surprising that he had an astounding number of friends and acquaintances. I thought it might be a mistake for me to live with Chris, but dismissed my doubts because I thought it was what Dan and Leigh wanted.

And so we were six. But Ruth and I were worried. We had lived through some wrenching changes, we had turned our lives upside down, we were raising Matt, and we wanted to live with some people whose understandings approximated those which we had so painstakingly accumulated. Chris, Leigh and Dan were all several years younger than we, they had been touched by radical politics, by drugs, by communal ideas while they were still in school. When we explained our concern Leigh became upset, she was sure we were saying she was immature, unworthy. But when Ruth and I mentioned Anne and Gary as people with whom we might like to live, Leigh and the others agreed to talk it over with them. We had only recently met Anne and Gary, but we had warmed to them quickly. When we called them up, they said they were thinking about living with Pete–a man we all knew. So we set a date for the nine of us to get together.

Arrangements

One spring evening we sat down in our living room and began to talk, keeping a lot of what we were thinking to ourselves, but no doubt revealing more than we intended. We had to see if we liked one another, whether we could talk like friends. And it was just as important to know if we all had similar ideas of what it would be like to live together. We had strangeness to overcome, and genuine differences in how we had been living and what we valued, and fears of judging as well as of being judged. The possibility that one of us might not live up to another's standards, that some body might have to say that he or she didn't want to live with somebody else there that night made for a hesitant, probing mood which prevailed every time we talked about our new house during the next few months.

I wanted to be accepting and understanding, and yet there was no way around looking at Pete or at Chris and wondering, can I live with that *stranger?* There were moments when I thought that it was crazy to be there altogether: swimming against the current of my culture required an unflagging resolve, lessons long ago learned broke over my consciousness like waves of doubt. To be sitting with people I hardly knew, speaking of sharing a home–a kitchen, a refrigerator, a bathroom. So much of what I am is symbolized by the details of my home, by the food I eat, the hair or lack of it in the bathroom sink–my home is an emblem of my aspirations. Just so. I accepted the doubt and indecision as among the less consequential costs of having decided to live in a group. But were these the right people? Except for Chris, who missed that first meeting, and Pete, with whom I had never really talked,I had begun to trust that everybody else would respect my sensitivities. And I was yearning for a home, the beginning of a future. I had decided that just like falling in love, picking your intentional family was largely a matter of luck, or instinctive trust in your own judgement: you played around and fenced around and waited to be excited, or comforted, or reassured, and in the end you guessed—yes or no—without ever knowing why.

Neither Gary nor Anne had ever lived in a commune before. For them, if they decided to chance it, it would be a leap into the unknown from four years of privacy, orderliness, and an increasingly involving marriage. They were, compared to Ruth and me, financially well-off—Gary was a doctor and Anne a teacher and they had a lot of furniture, books, records, paintings, artifacts, kitchenware, a car, a stereo system, a motorcycle. Anne had become interested in communal living before Gary, but by the time they arrived in Upper Darby that night in April, he was more enthusiastic. Anne thought that nobody would like her because she was too straight, too conventional. But she also knew precisely why she wanted to live with other people.

"I'm interested in living communally because I want more intimate relationships than just the one with Gary," she said in a voice that shook a little. "I want other people to help me grow, to help Gary grow, and to help us grow together. And politically I feel it's absurd for a person to have a car of their own, or their own couch."

She was blunt and spoke without embellishment. Eventually I learned that Anne sets out to get what she wants with a great force, a considerable will. What she was after was a happier life with Gary, and before long the rest of us would find ourselves enlisted in her campaign to get it.

Leigh was of two minds about Anne. She admired her outspokenness. But she was seven years younger than Anne, who was thirty-one, and she was worried about being excluded by the two older women. She could see how much Ruth and Anne liked each other, and she was afraid that they wouldn't respect the validity of her experience. So she kept testing, prodding them for reactions, especially Anne.

"I've always lived communally in a way," she said, thinking somewhat resentfully about how her father's house had been a harbor for his friends and patients. "I guess what I'm looking for is a situation where there's a lot of equality, where people don't get cast in one kind of role or another." This was directed toward Anne. It was both timid and a bit arch. "And a group that feels comfortable and supportive around what I'm doing in the women's movement and with anti-war stuff."

She thought she sounded defensive, and disliked herself for it.

Meanwhile, Dan was having his doubts about whether he could make a go of it with Gary and Anne, who seemed burdened by a lot of money and possessions and who had a certain intangible security, as well. He turned the conversation toward possessiveness.

"The only thing I own that I guess I don't want ripped off is my sleeping bag," he said nonchalantly, as if that were an unquestionably sound and customary point of view.

Pete was keeping pretty quiet, sitting back on his haunches and watching the give and take. He was afraid of Dan. Although they had met at any number of political meetings, Dan seemed young and uncompromising to him, and he was sure that Dan would eventually scorn his more comfortable, accepting ways.

But Dan was also the most easygoing person in the group sprawled around the room that night. He could drawl the laziest loops around the staccato city talk which the rest of us kept in motion. In this, though neither of them knew it at the time, he and Pete were very much alike. Months later Pete would say that he and Dan "anchor the non-psychological wing of the house."

"Well," Dan replied, when Gary asked him what he was looking for in a commune, "living with other people feels better. You have more fun with other people and you can always find people to do things with or get help. It felt good in a big family growing up."

Gary gave me the impression that night of being fidgety, eruptive. He kept running his long fingers through his thick, dark brown hair. For awhile he would say nothing, and then he'd' let loose a torrent of words. He was intimidated by me, by my long black hair and beard, by my having lived in a commune before. I appeared mysterious and vaguely dangerous to him, and he couldn't imagine why I'd want to live with him. He suspected that I really wanted to live with Anne, and that she might be sexually attracted to me, too. Though he thought that I was sensitive and intelligent, he dwelled within himself on my strong, even dogmatic manner.

As the night wore on there was less tension. We talked the same language. And we looked and dressed alike, which gave us some superficial reassurance. The men all had long hair, and the men and women alike wore dungarees and work shirts or T-shirts, boots or sneakers. Before the others went home we decided to go to the beach the next weekend. Gary and Anne wanted to bring along a friend who was also interested in living with us, and there were no objections.

That first night, and in the next few weeks Ruth and I felt responsible for helping the others to reconcile their differences. We had brought Chris, Dan, and Leigh together with Gary, Anne, and Pete, and in that sense we were pivotal. Ruth and I were also the only people in the group who had lived in a commune which could serve as a rough model for what most of us had in mind for our new house. So there was a disposition, especially on the part of Gary and Anne, to view us as being especially knowledgeable and wise.

Saturday morning, after a half-dozen phone calls and a chaos of plans made and altered and made again–a style of group confusion about doing something which has characterized us ever since–we piled into three cars and headed for the Jersey coast. Anne and I sat together in a back seat, talking rapidly and easily about our marriages. It was a gray, damp day. When we got to the ocean, we walked and ran along the beach, huddled together on blankets, threw around a

16

ball, and occupied the deserted dun and gray oceanside with our boisterous presence. I felt free and quick, loping along the sand, breathing deep gulps of the wet, salty air while the gulls glided and squawked overhead.

Having that fun together did more to loosen us up with one another than all the portentous talks in the world. I was really pleased. We bought a crateful of fresh New Jersey lobsters and a case of beer and headed back to Upper Darby where we tore into the food, blew off steam, shouted a lot and collided in tentative, friendly ways. Leigh, who was still wary of Gary, began to relax when the two of them made brownies in the middle of an incredible mess in the kitchen, and just acted loony together. They were both self-consciously restrained, but also enjoying each other.

Afterward, when we all sat down to talk again, Anne's friend Sharon included, our ease began to evaporate. Sharon's relationship to the rest of us was ambiguous because it appeared she was including herself in, and except for Gary and Anne nobody was at all certain that was okay.

After our day on the beach there seemed to be a subtle shift in our assumptions, as though the fun we had had together had made our intentions toward each other more explicit. It was like a courtship, yes, a group courtship. We had met and been attracted and so arranged a first date, which, though it had been awkward and unfamiliar, gave us enough promise of a possible future to warrant a day at the seashore. And there we had begun to laugh together. No passions were stirred yet, but we shared some sort of dawning recognition. At times, sudden personal discoveries broke past the bounds of propriety; at other times we bogged down in the sad, tense ambiguities of trying to make sure that we had the same future in mind.

Soon we began to talk about what Pete called arrangements, about conscious accommodations to what each of us wanted. And what a weighty load of subjects confronted us: money, possessions, sex, privacy, limits on our involvement, sex roles—in short, the politics of an intentional family. It was a marvelous opportunity, forming such an unconventional household. We were serious, we were truly disgusted with the way things were generally being done, and so we had all been swept into a restless seeking after more satisfying styles of existence; we were ready to begin deciding which cultural conditioning we could discard, which we wanted to shed but could not, and, finally, which values and behavior, like our own skins, wrapped us in forms which gave us coherence.

So there we were, timorous and anxious and friendly, beginning to talk about money. The Movement was pervasive: our politics provided us with an incentive for money sharing, and a framework for our decision, but wherever dogma intruded upon good sense there were unspoken pressures. Gary was a physician and Pete a doctor of science and both of them had incomes far larger than the rest of ours. They were sheepish: they hadn't sought privilege, but they had worked hard for what they wanted and were overcome by no burning desires to give away what they had earned. Meanwhile, Dan, Leigh, Ruth, Chris, and I were not only poorer than they were, but intimidating as well. Our political style was more that of activists; in addition, Dan had dropped out of medical school and I out of newspapering, both of us were temperamentally more anti-institutional than Gary, Pete, or Anne. The three of them all felt defensive about being too middle-class (sin of sins in 1971) as we talked about money arrangements. Nobody came out and said, "For chrissake, Gary, you've got no business being a doctor and making so much money," but silent doubts communicated themselves nonetheless.

The impetus for money sharing came from Ruth and me. We hadn't been sharing money with Gil and Wendy and the differences in our wealth had been a source of friction. Ruth and I earned less but felt that it would be greedy to suggest that we should contribute less than they. Gil and Wendy, meanwhile, felt that they were greedy in not offering to contribute a larger share of our expenses, but they were saving money in order to travel. By and large, we avoided talking about money except when it was absolutely necessary because we were all defensive. We just split all our bills fifty-fifty and left it at that. But Ruth and I had learned that friendliness could be eroded just as surely by being cautious about money sharing as by taking the risk of beyond the usual boundaries. I suggested to our new group that if there was a pool of shared income then decisions about how to spend it–basic decisions about our communal lifestyle–would be less inhibited by possessiveness. I said that my hope was that if I threw my money into a common kitty then I would view it less as an extension of me, and more as a commodity over which I had a shared control.

With Pete acting as bookkeeper, we all listed our anticipated incomes. Pete and Gary were both making about $15,000 a year, Dan was out of work, and I earned less than $2,000 a year from freelancing and other odds and ends. Anne was making about $10,000, and Ruth would be paid about $8,000 if the job she wanted came through. These differences in our incomes created two different kinds of problems. Chris, Dan, Leigh and I all wanted assurances from the people with larger earnings that we wouldn't be begrudged a share of their salaries. Leigh, in fact, was uncomfortable about being supported at all, but Health Information Project, which was just getting underway, could afford to pay her no more than a pittance–movement wages, we called it.

Meanwhile, the people with more substantial incomes had their own doubts. Gary was feeling intimidated, especially by Dan, who had dropped out of medical school to do political organizing, and whose whole situation seemed to comment unfavorably on Gary's more conventional life as a young, politically concerned doctor. But Gary couldn't be sure just what Dan thought about him because in a tight, highly pressured situation–and this was just that–Dan's opinions were vaguely and generally expressed. Every time Gary said something he thought might have violated Dan's standards, he waited for a reaction. But none came.

It was apparent that Gary, Anne, and Pete would be contributing a great deal of money under any kind of income sharing plan, that, in part at least, they would be supporting the group which approached them about living together. And, even though at that early point in our history there was some trust that money had not motivated our overture, we were all Americans, and nobody overcomes an American education about money simply by wishing it would go away. As we went on talking it seemed that we all thought income sharing was admirable, but also had reservations. Like my grandma says, money is honey. For an American there is nothing more passionately private, more fervently personal, more symbolically significant of success or failure. Money was divisive, it separated neighbors who would turn to ash before they discussed their incomes, it set spouses at odds–"Why should *I* wash the dishes? I earn the money around here, don't I?" But the eight adults in our group all held to an approximate political goal, we were all more or less anti-capitalist. We wanted to see the national wealth redistributed so that every American would have a reasonably similar and sufficient level of comfort. What better place to begin making those readjustments than in our own lives? How, after all, could we countenance a situation in which Chris–who made about eighteen hundred dollars teaching Greek and Latin in an alternative high school, and wasn't paid at all for helping to run a food co-op-would contribute the same amount to our house as Gary, whose fifteen-thousand-dollar salary was paid by the government?

Money, and the comforts and securities it brings, are important to everybody, everywhere. But capitalism–which public school teachers call the Free Enterprise System, as though calling it by its true name would be uncouth or embarrassing (in this it enjoys the same sacrosanct status as bowel movements, natural expulsions of gas, and sexual intercourse)–capitalism had taught us that what we have we win at the expense of others who are less successful at competing than we are. Capitalism seemed to be ultimately self-defeating. It had come to imply that money and goods were more important than the quality of life or the shared national experience, and so these were eroded by the sanctified pursuit of the buck. Our decision to reject capitalist values in our household by redistributing our wealth had a pleasing ring—we were using our money to express support for each other, for the kind of radical political work some of us were doing, and for our intentions toward each other.

We were also boggled by our combined income, which, while it was a good deal less than our potential earning power (all of us had college degrees, and half of us graduate degrees as well), was still much more than we needed to live on.

Together we were making about $50,000 a year before taxes and other deductions. We began to consider how much of our incomes to share, and in what fashion. Many rural communes, we knew, shared all their money, but most urban communes with which we were familiar didn't. In a rural setting where a group of people had cut themselves off entirely from their previous work and lifestyle, and where all their money came from their cooperative labor, then total money sharing was only logical. But the common sense of total money sharing wasn't as compelling in our situation, where we all worked at different occupations, and where our intention wasn't to begin a new life but rather to build a new home as part of our ongoing lives. We talked about a graduated scale with the people who made the most contributing a higher percentage, but we rejected that because it seemed too incautious a beginning. Finally we decided to try a plan under which each individual would put half of his or her earnings into a housefund and keep the other half for private use. We agreed that it would be a big step toward a feeling of collective existence, we would be pledging something more substantial than our benevolent intentions toward one another. It also safeguarded our autonomy by assuring each of us continued freedom to come and go within the limits of our incomes, by leaving us all some getaway money, and by guaranteeing each of us some measure of continued financial independence. And it seemed a cautious beginning, it didn't push us too rapidly past our actual limitations toward some ideal goal. Another consideration was that the six of us who were coupled off wouldn't be treated as appendages of each other; it would encourage us to treat one another as individuals and not in tandem, as married couples especially are usually treated.

Our plan was that the housefund would pay for rent, food, utilities, transportation and auto upkeep including insurance, all household expenses, and a ten-dollar-a-week allowance for each of the adults. The allowance was supposed to help us avoid situations where we might all want to do something together like go to a restaurant, but some people might not be able to afford it. We decided to pay for clothing out of our own pockets because we thought that how much clothing an individual had, and its quality, were too much matters of personal preference to be subject to collective control. We didn't want to find ourselves weighing a shirt somebody wanted against whether they truly needed it.

We agreed rather easily that we would support Matt collectively, and that if Gary and Anne had the kid they were planning we would also support their baby with group money.

Inherent in the entire agreement was an understanding that if one of the people with the higher incomes wanted to stop working after awhile, or wanted to change to a lower paying job, and if that created a need for more income, then one of us who had been indulged would be responsible for bringing in the extra that was needed.

What benefits did we envision? Well, we all felt virtuous doing something demanding and unusual just because we believed it was right. We were proud. And we thought that sharing half our incomes would enable us to live active, productive urban lives without always having primary responsibility either for making money or being a homemaker or both. We hoped to relieve the dependencies fostered by sex-role stereotyping in nuclear families, and to end the enforced loneliness of living in ones and twos: the pleasures and drudgeries of working, earning money, and caring for our own home were to be available to all of us equally.

We decided, too, that we would share the use and costs of the cars. And here Leigh enjoyed a certain ironic, private amusement. Nearly a year before, when she hardly knew him, she had just about bought Pete's Toyota, but then changed her mind at the last minute. Now, she smiled to herself, she would have the Toyota anyway, and without laying out a penny. It would be months before she was confident that Pete could enjoy the humor without resenting the truth of what had happened. In addition to the Toyota, our cars included a Volvo which Ruth and I owned, Leigh's Mercedes diesel, and Gary and Anne's Volkswagen.

We also acknowledged the existence of private property, of items each of us possessed that we didn't want to become common property. Gary and Anne were outspoken about this, and it made me wonder if they were really ready to go as far into communality as I thought I wanted to. They had more possessions than any of the rest of us, and seemed more emotionally attached to them. Still, all of us had some things we wanted to keep out of the way of harm and wear. For me, there was my typewriter, a fifteen-year-old Smith-Corona desk model. I've been talking to myself by pounding on it for a long, long time, and I want it to be with me for a long time more. When a key broke not so long ago I felt as though some vital vessel in a loved one had burst.

Our conversation about money and possessions lasted a long, exhausting night. At its end, we were all drained by the cautious, judgement-ridden negotiations, and by our private doubts. We still reserved the right to pull out, but turning back had become more difficult than going ahead: it to me that we were half-willingly snaring ourselves into living together. Just before we broke up Gary said that he knew about a seven-bedroom house in Germantown which was up for rent.

Pete drove home that night very unsettled. The group was moving perilously close to an agreement, and he still wasn't sure whether or not he wanted to be part of it. He was uncertain about giving up his car and half his income to group use. It scared him just to think about it. His family had had very little, and he had worked hard for everything he had acquired. For years he had an almost Scottish stinginess, it had been hard for him to get accustomed to having and spending money on himself. Finally, though, he had disciplined himself to enjoy the life he could afford, and now he felt endangered by agreeing to give any of it away, especially to people whom he hardly knew and who were earning nothing or very close to it by their own choice. And yet he also knew that he was lonely, that for years he had talked and thought about living in a commune. He knew he would have to make a decision–and soon. And he knew too that he was thirty-five years old, and that this was probably the last opportunity he would have to live in a commune, that either he would join this group or very probably would never join any. Perhaps what eventually tipped the balance for him was knowing that Gary and Anne had many of the same doubts, that, if need be, they could huddle together and give each other succor in the new house. The new house! He really would just about start shaking when he said that, even to himself.

* * *

About a week later, in a more relaxed mood, we talked about Matt. Anne, who had been teaching kids for nine years, was starting to like Matt. Sometimes she thought he was spoiled and bratty, but at other times she was amazed by how articulate he was, and how sensitive to other people. There was the time when she had been nearby when he leaned over and kissed a boy friend and said, "There! I did it! I've been wanting to do that for the longest time." Anne could see, too, that I had a lot of guilt about raising Matt in such crazy-quilt homes, and so sometimes withheld clearcut decisions when he needed them. She wondered what was the best relationship between Matt and the other adults, and what Ruth and I would want.

We told the other people that we intended to go on being Matt's only parents, but that we hoped they would become his friends and assume some responsibility for his well-being. That came very close to what most of the other adults wanted, too. Again, Pete was baffled, there seemed to be just one unknown prospect after another. He had very little idea of what living with an eight-year-old might really entail. Pete thought of Matt as just a cute little grown-up kid, not as a separate person.

I was reluctant to put Matt into a situation where he would be the only child among eight grownups, but I was even more reluctant to live just the three of us on his account, and then spend years thinking how grateful he should feel for all I had given up in his behalf. No, I wouldn't do that. But I went on doubting the decision Ruth and I had made, wondering if it was fair. I felt quite vulnerable in a way that nobody else in the group did, except for Ruth.

The question of Matt's being the only child in our group was incidental to Ruth's decision. She had looked for people with whom she wanted to live, and when she found them none of them had any kids. She wondered why not, why so few of the people she was closest to had children. It made her feel lonely.

*   *   *

We didn't talk about sex until after we had rented the house on Cliveden street several weeks later and were already decided on living together.

"There`s something I have to talk about," Gary Said when we were all sitting around one night. "I haven`t brought it up before because I was afraid of seeming too old-fashioned or something." There was a nervous pause. "It's that I'm very jealous about Anne's and my sexual relationship. It's not something I want to expand or share, and I'm worried that other people in the house might try to get us to break that down." His voice was a trifle reedy, and he sat cross-legged on the floor, looking agitated. At the back of his mind was his first college romance–he had broken it off when the girl had slept with another man, causing him agonies of rage and pain, like a fire in the pit of his stomach.

Ruth sighed audibly, but said nothing. "Well, monogamy is an issue that Dan and I are struggling around," Leigh said, trying to gather her thoughts. Gary so often emphasized his privacy and his fears that she thought he wouldn't ever push her to explore her own limits. "I can respect your decision about your own relationship," she said. "I don't want you to feel any pressure from me to change that if you don't want to."

I was drawn to Anne, and I immediately felt at a loss about how to sort out my feelings in this situation.

"You know Ruth and I have been talking about the possibility of sleeping with other people," I said cautiously. "But getting involved with somebody else in the house seems a little too frighteningly immediate and close to me."

"I think I'd feel best," said Ruth, who had fantasized about making love with Dan, "if we could reach an agreement that nobody would sleep with anybody else in the house outside of the couples who are already together."

"Why's that?" Dan asked sweetly and curiously.

"Because I think I'd feel a lot safer like that, too," said Anne. She was thinking not only about Gary, but about the appeal that Pete, Dan, and I had for her. But her investment was steep, and she intended to protect it. "I feel old-fashioned and everything," she said, "but that's just where I'm at."

Chris, meanwhile, was intensely uncomfortable. The level of sexual feeling and uncertainty in the room was high, but he knew that this was the time to broach what he was thinking about.

"I'm really worried about bringing this up," he said in a small, soft voice, "but I want to be sure that everybody knows I'm gay and is sure that's okay with them." And he waited for the axe to fall.

But it didn't. The men who had never lived with Chris or any other homosexual before–Pete, Gary and I–all had pretty similar responses. We each said that we found Chris' sexuality a threat, and that we weren't interested in having sex with another man, and we thought that living with Chris would force us to confront ourselves more directly than we had.

Gary asked Chris why he was willing to live in a heterosexual group.

"Well, I didn't especially into consideration when I decided who I wanted to live with," Chris said. "I wanted to live with this group of people because of who they are, not because they're gay or straight." He anticipated that what problems he would have would show themselves subtly, in how people said things, in their attitudes and reactions.

I thought Chris' answer was incomplete, but was reluctant to say so. His decision raised questions about his own sexuality to which I would have liked some more answers, but I was sufficiently unsure of myself–and of him–to press him.

There was something else on Chris' mind which was even more difficult for him to bring up.

"I want to be sure that Mike and Ruth feel all right about my taking care of Matt, like if I'm ever alone with him, babysitting or something," he said in a choked voice.

I reached over and grabbed Chris' hand and said that I trusted him; Ruth came across the room and hugged him. I was angry, incensed at our culture for having taught us to so thoroughly fear homosexuality that a line, gentle man like Chris couldn't trust himself or be sure he would be trusted around a boy child. But I was angry at myself, too, because I knew that his concern wasn't unfounded: I was worried that if Matt found out that Chris was gay, he would be upset. I trusted Chris to be alone with Matt, but there was nothing in anybody else's sex life I wanted to protect Matt from knowing about, I only wanted him to be taught with sensitivity. In Chris' case, I wasn't sure I wanted him to be taught at all.

Many, many months later Matt, who by that time was aware that other men sometimes shared Chris' bed, asked Pete and Ruth and me while all of us were in the kitchen on Cliveden street: "What's a homosexual?"

"That's a man who makes love with other men," I answered after a pause and an exchange of glances among the other adults.

A moment later Matt left the kitchen, his curiosity apparently satisfied.

*   *   *

One evening in early summer we all gathered at Gary and Anne's apartment to go to a Chinese restaurant. Just before we were about to leave, Dan said it would be nice to be stoned.

"I've got some grass that Anne's Uncle Berle grew himself," Gary said cordially, "but it's pretty good stuff and if we smoke a joint we may not be going anywhere for a while."

I had been smoking grass for years but had never known dope so strong that one joint would have much impact on nine or ten people, so I was pretty dubious. Gary went upstairs and fetched a tiny little stash in a plastic bag and then somebody rolled a fat joint which we passed around. Everybody got two hits, maybe some people got three. The next thing I remember is that Gary was standing on a chair trying to rouse us into motion, that I was lolling on the floor laughing at the urgency of his gestures but not making much sense out of his words, and that people were splattered all over the floor and furniture. A couple of hours later we left for the restaurant where we ordered a large, exotic Mandarin meal, passing each course around. Then we went back to the apartment and smoked some more.

The lights were out and a record was playing which I later found out was Happy and Artie Traum's first album (that record eventually became our house favorite, and we the only Happy and Artie groupies in Christendom), and I kept fading in and out of the music and the room. I was sitting on a rocker and swaying slightly. Anne was stretched out on her back on a fur rug with her dark blond hair spread around her head. She was wearing a beige turtleneck sweater, and I thought, at that moment, that she was the softest, the roundest, the most desirable woman I had ever seen. I would look at her and grow dizzy with desire, and then, with a start, think–how the hell am I going to deal with this? and then I would get lost in the music or the flame of a candle. Everybody was lost in their own thoughts and dreams. After awhile Gary got up in the middle of the room and began to dance and shout. I sensed that his display was directed at me. What the hell was this? I tried to get up and dance too, but my muscles were oozing like jelly and it felt safer back in the rocker than on my feet. I got

28

lost again, and then Gary came over to me and said he'd like to talk, so we walked into the kitchenette off the living room and he starting talking to me with great urgency about his older brother, who had dominated him and pushed him around and whom he loved very much. He said that his relationship with his brother repeated itself with other strong men. with whom he always felt fiercely competitive. Men like me, he said.

Pete was sitting across the room on the couch watching us, amused at what looked to him like the two largest males in the group trying to establish dominance. "There's real interesting times ahead between them two big boys," he smiled to himself.

Gary's outpouring was sweeping away what little equilibrium I had, and I put all my effort into trying to understand his words and remain agreeable. I was overwhelmed by the surge of energy he was directing at me, by the insistence that I deal with him. Finally he clasped me in his arms and I hugged back–a bearish embrace–glad that this scene seemed to be drawing to its conclusion. I didn't understand why we were hugging, but I knew that it was what Gary wanted, and I was impressed by his courage and determination. But I was also feeling invaded by the whirlwind of his emotions, so I was both attracted and repelled. When I knew Gary better I began to see how often he had been successful at getting what he wanted, how relentless he was, but also how he had enough confidence to be considerate and gentle as well.

The whirlwind that Gary was creating was really the of times to come. The Berle weed (we saved the seeds and planted them in the backyard the next spring) had knocked down enough inhibitions so that sexual fantasies, craziness and some of our deepest instincts to reach out for comfort and understanding were unleashed. Now we were ready to move.

But there was still one intolerably unresolved matter, Anne's friend Sharon. Whenever she was with us there was a special uneasiness. Her lifestyle seemed different enough to cause unnecessary problems if we lived together. I thought

that she could be both clinging and vindictive, in fact had seen
her be both when pushed. We talked when she wasn't there
and found that most of us didn't want to live with her. It was
time for somebody to tell her, but nobody did. Finally, one
afternoon, Ruth and I happened to run into her when we were
picking up Anne at the community school where she taught.
We all went back to our place together, where we talked
around it for a long while, and in the end I said the hurtful
thing which had to be said. Later I told Gary and Anne that
they should have handled it sooner, and by themselves.

I've learned that I can't live with everybody I like, that the
basis on which I form friendships sometimes differs from how
I make living bonds. It's difficult to be precise about the
differences. Maybe there are characteristics which I can
readily enough accept in people I like, but which would be too
disruptive in the people with whom I live. Friends who are
abrasively blunt or in whom I sense an insistence on argument
come to mind. I want to be at my ease where I live. As much
as it's my intention in living with other people to become
engaged, I also need to feel that they will accord my
vulnerabilities and my peace of mind a great deal of
sensitivity. I don't want to be confronted by problems at every
turn, either somebody else's or my own. Where I live and the
people who live there with me are my home. Perhaps it's an
unusual, even a bizarre home. Certainly it's experimental and
probably it won't endure. Nevertheless, I'm not eager to be
pushing out at all my limits to see how far I can stretch. It
must be exclusive as well as inclusive.

*   *   *

Well, moving day finally arrived. We rented a twenty foot
van, borrowed a smaller truck from a friend, and lit into it.
First we cleaned out our house in Upper Darby. What a huge
collection of junk we cart around with us! Slowly I am moving
toward whatever will constitute my essentials, some few
things chosen for their beauty and their utility.

We Schlepped our truckfuls of junk and treasure out to the new house, unloaded it all, and the next morning headed for Gary and Anne's place. Their couch was too big to get down the stairs, so using a borrowed hoist and some heavy rope, we lowered it out of the second-floor window with a great commotion. I was dancing around in the street with my arms stretched above my head while this seemingly giant couch headed straight down toward me. I expected that any minute I'd be crushed like a big, black waterbug—just what I deserved for this entire escapade. Half the neighbors on the block seemed to be out digging the show, and up on the corner a bunch of kids had opened a hydrant and let loose a torrent of water, which they aimed at cars and buses driving by. The rest of us ignored their pranks, but Gary Walked up to the corner and earnestly told them to cut it out.

By Saturday afternoon we were moved in, but after a fashion. The house was filled with dressers, chairs, clothes, books, records, kitchenware and cartons full of what my grandma calls *bupkus* and *hazarai*. What a jumble. Pete stood and looked it over, fighting the impulse to turn right around toward the security of his nice little Center City apartment with the brick wall.

Sunday morning bright and early Ruth and I had our car loaded and with Matt we struck off toward Alaska for six weeks. It would be nearly Labor Day before all nine of us were together in the house. A long pause for summer, and then we would begin in earnest.

Our House

The house was built in 1904 with stone walls eighteen inches thick. There's a towering copper beech standing just west of the house where the yard runs up the short side of the property before it sweeps back deep behind the rear. Two hundred years ago when Roger Sherman of Connecticut was asked to dedicate a bridge he walked its length, and then said "I don't see but it stands steady." His words do just fine to describe my feelings about our place.

Matt's best friend Jono told me a while ago that, "You always smell like your house." When I walk up the three wide concrete steps and through the white portal into the front hall what I smell is: food cooking, my dog Gus, dampness from those thick stone walls, and fire or soot from the fireplaces in the dining room on my left and the living room on my right. Jono said he liked the smell. If it`s fall or winter or early spring there's likely to be a lire lit in the living room, giving it a certain coziness despite its size. WW often there's music playing, too. American folk or bluegrass music, Mozart, Bach, Vivaldi, Handel. Rock 'n' roll. The floor is covered with an ivy green carpet left behind by the owner, and above the fireplace a white tile mantle runs straight up to the twelve-foot ceiling. The wall on either side of the fireplace is wood-paneled. Once that whole length of the room was thirty-five feet of French doors leading to a verandah, but two owners back some jerk built on a garage and closed off that access to the outdoors, replacing brick, stone and glass with cement, tile and paneling.

The rear wall of the living room–to your left as you enter–is bookshelves painted white. In the middle of the shelves there's a door, the top of which is a window leading to an enclosed back porch where we stacked the four cord of firewood we burned that first winter. Not long after we moved in Ruth was sitting alone in the living room when she heard somebody nearby huffing and puffing, a remarkable and mysterious noise. She stood up and began to look for its source and finally she found Dan out there on the back porch lifting weights, barechested, and she watched for a minute as the muscles of his chest and arms flowed with the strain of hoisting and lowering the weight, but then she became embarrassed by her rising warmth. Like the rest of us, she was still fighting against the sexuality of her responses to the people in the house. So she went back inside and put a record on the stereo which sat on a heavy, dark oak table just beside the bookshelves on the far side of the room.

In the center of the room there's a couch, a soft over stuffed chair and ottoman, a corduroy seated rocker, a round leather-topped coffee table, and a couple of lamps. The front of the room–facing the bookshelves–has two large windows and a table cluttered with some of the stuff we read: *Village Voice, Mother Earth News, New England Journal of Medicine, New York Review of Books, Communitas, Zap Comix, Ramparts, New York Times Magazine*, sheet music for Chris' recorder and for the guitars.

Gary loves to sit in the living room, sunk into the big, soft chair, listening to classical music on the earphones, reading a book. It was just a month or two after he had begun to live on Cliveden street that he was sitting there one night while a bunch of us had gone to see John Korty's movie River run, sitting there with his eyes closed, the book resting open on his lap, getting in touch with how much he had missed this kind of delicious quiet and solitude, recalling the fun he had had rough-housing with Matt earlier in the evening, before tucking him into bed, thinking how the richness of living with a child was so much more rewarding than, and so different from, what he had imagined . . . .

. . . when Ruth walked into the room. She was wearing an aqua caftan, she had just washed her hair and it was tied up in a towel. She stood watching Gary, his long legs stretched out resting on the ottoman, wearing blue jeans that stopped two inches above his sneakers, so that a slash of white sweat sock was showing. His feet, his knees, his elbows were all knobby, they angled out from the Hat planes of his torso. But what struck her most sharply was the look of concentration on his face, even in repose. She walked quietly out of the room again, just before Gary, sensing her presence, and feeling both annoyed at the interruption and glad for the company, opened his eyes to find that the room was empty.

Gary shut his eyes again and smiled, delighted that he was still alone. But just then the door bust open and he was brushed by a chill draft as Leigh, Chris, Anne, and I all rushed in, chattering and laughing, and filling what had been his solitary space with liking and noise. And it was perfectly all right—that surprised him, how all right it was, in fact—so he took off the earphones and joined the rest of us in the kitchen where we were all raiding the refrigerator and talking about the movie. He ate three Oreo cookies and drank a glass of cold milk and liked himself a whole lot.

And the other person I associate most vividly with the living room is Chris, sitting at the table at 3 A.M. surrounded by a pile of Greek and Serbian texts which he is reading intently while drawing on a small hookah in the glow of a single lamp, a crushed Kleenex at his elbow.

Across the foyer, the dining room is papered in red brocade and dominated by a twelve-foot table Pete and Leigh built. The other door out of the dining room leads you toward the back of the house, through a pantry, past the first-floor bathroom, and into the kitchen. Behind the kitchen is a laundry room, and a tiny, sunny storage room.Just outside one of its wall-length windows a cardinal built her nest, while we looked on, noses pressed to the glass.

Up the broad, carpeted steps is the second-floor hall, a square space oil of which are four bedrooms and a bath. As the year began, the first room on the right was a common room.

34

We put a stereo in there and book shelves and some beat-up old easy chairs, all of them sitting on a domestic Oriental rug with a dark gray field. Don and Leigh were sharing the front room across the hall. But Leigh began to feel crowded like that, her relationship with Dan was undecided, and she began to resent the automatic assumption that couples would share a room.

Leigh decided that she needed a place of her own, a sanctuary. She had always found it necessary to light for her right to be herself on her own terms, and so had grown up with a hardworking devotion to whatever task she undertook and a muted but unshakable dedication to opposing injustice. Her father, a charming, mercurial, and brilliant psychoanalyst, had been married three times before she was an adolescent; the imposition of his personal life undoubtedly influenced not only her desire for privacy, but her fragile trust of men, as well.

She met Dan when he asked her if she wanted to dance during a street fair in Rittenhouse Square in 1969. He was a tall, lanky young man with curly brown hair and a closely trimmed beard. She noticed right away that he was wearing a Resistance button. He looked like what he was: Pennsylvania Dutch being transformed by the city. That same night Leigh invited him back to her apartment, got him stoned, and went to bed with him. What fantasies Dan must have entertained of this sweet, self-assured city girl. Back home, near Lebanon, Pa., in a Church of Christ community where Jesus fulfilled your emotional needs, where you bathed only on Saturday night but washed your feet every other night to keep the bedsheets clean, where it was a good life peopled with a dozen brothers and sisters, where everybody worked hard, long days to provide enough food, back home in that harmonious, encapsulated world they hadn't prepared the bright, college-bound second son for what he'd find when he went to medical school in the big city: hadn't prepared him for the concrete squeezing out sky and grass, for the black people with the bushy hair and the bullhorns roaming the Penn campus sounding the call to insurrection, for the doctors who talked more about money than about curing, for the dope, the movies, the shoulder-length hair on men, the crazy, exhilarating radical ideas which–aagh, this was, at last, *too* much–made sense.

Dan's readiness for what he found in the city he attributed to a philosophy professor at his rural, denominational college who, quite simply and innocently, sounded the first inharmonious note in Dan's life by being an unmistakably good and gentle man who didn't accept Jesus. How hungry for new ideas and new ways Dan must have been if the impact of one sincere disbeliever could send such deep shudders through the foundations laid so painstakingly by family, by school, by church and by community.

It didn't take long after Dan and Leigh met for them to decide to share an apartment. But of course they shared more than that, together they postulated a world view, a focal point for their energy, their dissatisfaction, their dedication and their growth together. Health institutions and the revolution were the boundaries of their new world. They would go to demonstrations and get gassed, they met like-minded people from all around the country. Dan, especially, began to see himself as a fugitive, on the fringes.

In October Dan moved out of the room they had shared, leaving it to Leigh, and into the room at the top of the stairs. Perhaps the strongest impression he made on his new room was one of incompleteness: he hung burlap over one wall and got some brightly colored cloth for the ceiling, but never put it up. The room is littered with hints of his whims and cares: weights, medical texts, a marijuana plant growing on the window sill, copper plating, tools and a soldering iron, candy bars, and Baba Ram Dass' book *Be Here Now,* which Dan studied all winter long.

Leigh's room, across the hall, is cozy. It has a bright red carpet, window plants, a fireplace and shelves full of books, many of them about the women's movement. There is a large desk and a typewriter at which she works.

Pete's room is next to Leigh's. A friend described it as having the air of a monastery, but though it is cloistered and austere, it gives no hint of deprivation. One window looks east and in the morning the sun rises behind the tall trees which line the border of the backyard, and the light falls on Pete where he sleeps in a sturdy bed he built for himself. His hardwood floor is uncovered except for a small throw rug. There is a fireplace, a standing globe, a desk and a bureau.

His backpack hangs on a peg on the wall (in the garage he has a motorcycle and a ten-speed bicycle-Pete always leaves himself lots of escape routes). On an orange poster which faces his bed is the picture of a Vietnamese woman with a gun slung across her shoulder and the words of Ho Chi Minh:

The wheel of the law turns
without pause
After the rain, good weather
In the wink of an eye
The universe throws off
its muddy clothes
For ten thousand miles
the landscape spreads out like a beautiful brocade
Light breezes. Smiling flowers
High in the trees, amongst
the sparkling leaves
All the birds sing at once
Men and animals rise up reborn
What could be more natural?
After sorrow, comes joy.

When Pete talks about his past, there is a fine edge of bitterness to the recollections which make me think he harbors uncharted realms of anger. He was a loner who disliked the Jewish drugstore cowboys in his neighborhood, who almost flunked out of college and, spurring himself on, ended up doing post-doctoral work in Sweden, where he was on his own for the first time. His disrespect for authority borders on contempt. But with people he likes he is endlessly tolerant.

Ruth and I share the fourth bedroom, which we painted white with cream-colored woodwork. A kingsize bed with a multicolored quilt sits smack in the middle of the room. I light a fire on winter days to keep me warm when I'm working. In summer, the windows stand open. There's a desk in one corner with my typewriter on it, and a big, Indian print bedspread covers the wall behind our bed. From above the mantle a poster of a Galapagos tortoise looks down on us: wise old eyes. Over my desk are photographs of Ruth, Matt, and me taken by a friend. The one of Ruth shows a gentle-featured, thoughtful woman of medium height standing on a hillside in the woods. Her hands are thrust deep into the pockets on her wool poncho, and she is smiling, enjoying herself privately. Anticipation flickers at her slightly open mouth, reveals itself in the tilt of her head.

It took her longer, but like Leigh, Ruth eventually wanted a room of her own, too. Living in apartments we had always shared a bedroom, but we had both had other rooms in which it was easy to be alone. Now, though, she found herself in a houseful of people without any place that was just hers, and hers alone. As her work, her friendships, and the adjustments to our commune became more demanding, she craved some greater isolation. But that desire brought with it its own tensions, because she found that when she was alone she felt left out of what might be going on among other people in the house; but by winter she was often exhausted, drained and so had to be alone–and left out–a lot.

Remaining true to yourself and yet also being responsive to the group and its demands is a continual problem in our commune. Anne experienced it as wanting to be every body's center of attention, and wanting more privacy, too. It was especially difficult for couples. Like Ruth and me, Gary and Anne shared a large room up on the third floor, which led Anne to complain at a house meeting that, "I don't have any space that's just mine–except maybe the left side of our bed."

Boundaries are real and necessary living nine folks to one house. Sometimes, of course, they break down in such silly, unexpected ways that we have to laugh at ourselves. It was that way when Ruth, Leigh, and I found that we were all using the blue toothbrush in the second-floor bathroom cup because each of us thought it was ours. But by and large some simple rules seem to have evolved. Probably the most important is that a closed door is to be respected. The need to be all by yourself, with your aloneness uninterrupted, is crucial to maintaining your equanimity in our house, where intimacy is an explicit group value. It was hard at first, but necessary, to tell people to scram without worrying that you were hurting their feelings. As time goes on I continue to worry, but I'm better at staking out what territorial privacy I need. That involves not only situations where one person wants to be solitary, but also conversations which aren't open to whoever wanders by. Living together doesn't make us all equally friendly and intimate, all our relationships don't have an equal depth, concern, empathy, love. During the first year, for instance,I grew closer to Gary and Anne than to anybody else, and there were times when I wanted to be able to talk alone with just one or both of them. In the same way, I was excluded from Pete's and Leigh's friendship at times, and from Ruth's and Anne's and so on. When I was left out I tried to accept that, but at times jealousy and paranoia were inevitable.

Not long after we were in the house we also talked about establishing an individual's right to use the common rooms privately from time to time, especially the living room. We agreed that if you were in the living room either by yourself or with somebody else and you didn't want to be interrupted, that desire for privacy had to be respected. Despite this agreement, I still was hesitant about excluding people and sometimes copped out entirely by not saying when I felt intruded upon. And so it worked out that if you wanted privacy you usually headed for your bedroom, and if you shared a bedroom you were never guaranteed a private place, although as often as not you could find one.

I missed the whole days and evenings I had spent alone with Ruth and Matt before we moved into a commune, a quiet, familial happiness which wasn't duplicated except for the rare times when we were the only people home. To be alone as a family we would have to go out—or into our bedroom, but that wasn't the same as having an apartment to ourselves.

Gary and Anne both escaped a lot to their room on the third floor. Theirs was by far the largest bedroom, with tiny deep-set windows at both ends, one overlooking the front and the other the backyard. Their bed was covered by a hand-sewn Pennsylvania Dutch quilt, and their room, like ours, was usually neat. Most of their furniture was antique hardwood, and much more expensive than what anybody else owned. There was a rocker which Anne had restored, throw rugs, bookcases, a bedside lamp, and a cumbersome file case in which Gary saved everything.

Being on the third floor–which was the quietest and least crowded in the house–gave Gary some of the solitude he needed. He thought of himself as a private person who was presented with a basic tension living in a houseful of people, but he consoled himself by remembering that since he had chosen to live on Cliveden street whatever adjustments were necessary were also possible and within his control. "I look at it this way," he told me, "The option to sit alone and read, or listen to music, is really an option. I can always be with other people."

Moving down the house-length third-floor hall you pass Gary's darkroom, a big storage closet, the bathroom, and then you arrive at Chris' room. It took him two months to be finished working on it and ready to move into it. Paint was scraped and wood sanded and restored; plant racks were built in the window alcoves; low bookshelves erected, the floor sanded. There's a pigeon-hole desk crammed full of stuff, and a mattress on the floor. Everything is covered with something else: books, papers, tile cards, clothes, beads, trinkets, letters, shoes. To me, it looks like the aftermath of a tornado. But to Chris my room seems too sterile and orderly to be comfortable.

Matt's room is at the western end of the house. It's small, but has a nook and a sloped ceiling. Kid clutter: toys, paints, brushes, crayons, buttons and beads, string, a quarter, clothes, tools, a dismantled clock, a broken tape recorder fished out of a garbage pail, empty dishes and glasses, a deck of thirty-seven cards, rock collection, baseball cards, books, record player, records, record jackets. A bed, with a red and blue checked comforter crocheted by Ruth.

"I don't see why I have to clean up my room," Matt said whenever a grownup complains. "Nobody has to go in there.

I'm used to my room. I like it the way I like it. It's easier to find things in a messy room because you can see everything."

House Meeting

I stepped out of my room in the morning, headed for the bathroom, and bumped into Pete, orange hair and beard, wrapped in a yellow and black checked towel, built like a former high-school tailback. After you. No, no, after you. Our relationship was a pause: we were both waiting, our patience tempered by competitiveness, wariness, liking and self-doubt.

Routines were evolving in the house. Gary was the first one up and away in the morning, usually departing on his motorcycle before I was out of bed. Ruth, Leigh, and Anne left next. By eight Ruth was gone, just about the time I arrived in the kitchen. Eggs were usually sizzling in a frying pan, bowls on the kitchen table might be full of Pete's granola or Matt's Cap'n Crunch, and somebody might have made orange juice. I was reading Adele Davis and usually would set the blender buzzing into a concoction of milk, powdered milk, an egg, wheat germ, soy lecithin, and fruit. Water for tea or coffee was burbling on the stove. For me, at that hour, grunts and gestures substitute for conversation. Other people chattered away about the day's plans, about who needed a car and who was planning to cook supper and what they would make.

It was a trial for Leigh to get herself together in the morning. Pete watched as she left her pocketbook in the bathroom, her sandals on the landing, some papers in the dining room. She would start out toward the car, and then, just when she seemed to have gathered herself together and be on her way, she'd tear back in looking for the one thing she'd forgotten, stomping and cursing. It reminded him of how she spread herself thin, involving herself in what seemed to be a ceaseless round of meetings and activities, as if she forbade herself ever to say no.

Many mornings I helped Matt get ready for school, although Pete and Chris also took turns. Matt really liked his new school, which was run by parents and staff and which allowed him more freedom of expression and choice than he had ever encountered before. But he was having trouble making friends on our block, where he was the only white kid. And in the adult excitement of getting acquainted he was sometimes being overlooked.

Helping Matt get going in the morning began to deepen Pete's understanding of the special life of a child. At times he felt appreciative of the new responsibilities; at other times he felt defeated. He began to see that Matt, sleepy headed, slow-moving, strong-willed and stubborn in the early morning, responded best when Pete laid out what he wanted as clearly and unequivocally as possible. He learned to say, "You make a peanut butter and jelly sandwich for your lunch while I soft boil an egg for your breakfast." Matt was so remarkably grown-up that at first Pete had left him to fend for himself some mornings. But after awhile he saw how lonely it was to be eight years old and scrounging around by yourself for breakfast, so he began always keeping Matt company. At a house meeting Pete told the rest of us what he was learning about Matt; after awhile it wasn't uncommon for a portion of most meetings to be devoted to anecdotes and observations about Matt, sometimes with him there, and sometimes not. Meanwhile Pete and Matt were beginning to have good times together taking long rides into the country on Pete's motorcycle, or going out to a farm to ride the horse.

After Matt left for school Pete moved deliberately, sitting in the sunny backyard, working into a rhythm before he left for his laboratory. During the first few weeks of September Pete's friend Stella from San Francisco stayed with us. Stella had lived in a commune for years, and flowed easily into the newly cut riverbed of our lives together, under standing when to get out of the way, and when to pitch in and help; she created expectations that no other guest has lived up to. Guests who don't cook or clean or contribute some help, and who don't know how to make themselves scarce upon occasion, are not welcomed back though they sometimes return.

As for me, I was full of ambition, but largely inert. I wanted to start a newspaper for men, but couldn't enlist much support either among the men in my consciousness raising group or in the house. I went to work for our new food co-op, and met several times with a group that was planning a citywide radical weekly newspaper which never materialized. I wrote a couple of articles. Overall, though, I was impatient with myself, feeling disengaged and purposeless, earning almost no money and heading toward what appeared to be a barren winter, except for the excitement of living in the house. I was still very much a hound dog sniffing out the trail to my future, barking up a lot of the wrong trees, and at night, baying mournfully under the moon.

Anne was the first person in the house with whom I began to exchange confidences. One night, when I wanted to talk, We went out to get her a pack of cigarettes and returning, Sat for hours in the VW talking, not re-entering the house, stirred by being alone in the dark, close to each other, but scrupulously avoiding any kind of flirtation. During the summer she had become pregnant; then, just before returning to Cliveden street after a raft trip on the Colorado River, she had miscarried while visiting her folks in Los Angeles. The miscarriage had thrown her deeply into herself. Some of the dissatisfaction that separated her from Gary was close to the surface as we talked in the car. She was sure that she wanted to work out her problems with him, but not as confident that they would be able to establish the kind of marriage she wanted. She was asking herself whether or not the marriage could continue unless it changed to her satisfaction, and finding that she didn't know the answer. "It's a big if," she said, and she sounded frightened.

Anne had been raised to be a Jewish Princess, and in fact had become the May Queen of Fairfax High before going on to the University of Arizona because she had been advised it was the right kind of school for a pretty girl. When Arizona wasn't challenging enough, she transferred to UCLA, broke off an engagement because she could see the marriage would be unhappy in just the same ways her parents' was, went into Jungian therapy, and at twenty-two, accustomed to always maintaining appearances, started to dress sloppily, sleep around, and let the rebelliousness that had always been there finally take command. She was living happily by herself when she and Gary met. They were soon determined, each in their own way, to have each other, and after that was accomplished their determination was applied to making their marriage work. While they lived in a succession of apartments in a succession of cities there was as much separating as wedding them. Though Anne hesitated, though she thought she was too straight of style to be accepted in a commune, too crooked of purpose to make a go of it, she nonetheless decided to risk it, looking for help for her and for Gary, looking for a way of life which complemented her values, looking, most of all, for what ever it was that she wanted.

Before very long Gary's and Anne's problems would engage the rest of us. We had decided to meet once a week as a group, to hold house meetings. First of all, it seemed necessary in order to run a cooperative household, the nuts and bolts of communal living–schedules, chores, money and bank accounts, complaints, requests, cars, guests–all of these needed frequent attention. We also wanted to stay in touch with one another's lives. Coming and going as busily as a lot of us did offered scant guarantee that we would ever spend an evening all together. But most importantly, we wanted to have a setting for acting on our intention to talk about our concerns and problems, to seek sympathy, understanding, and advice from one another, to begin to build, in a conscious way, a network of engagement. After all, if living alone and in pairs had been sufficiently satisfying, none of us would have chosen to live with a group. We sought the company of other people, yes, but wanted something far more binding, too. Monday nights were set aside for house meetings, and for an entire year we didn't miss a week: our faithfulness to each other was unswerving. Very soon we learned that the kind of life we hoped to build together would probably be impossible without the meetings–they were like a pressure release, the place where you could most safely let off steam. Nothing was allowed to get in the way: we removed the phones from their hooks, and told our friends not to come over.

We were so wound up for our first meeting, so tentative and prickly, that nothing memorable happened. A week later, though, we were ready to try again. After dinner Pete headed straight for the kitchen to do the dishes, a much safer place, so far as he was concerned, than the living room where the rest of us were supposed to be going. In fact, the nervous desire to avoid the house meeting was at work in all of us. Gary picked just that time to get a screwdriver and begin working on the stereo. Chris was concentrating so intently on a book you might have needed dynamite to blast him loose from those protective pages. Ruth was crocheting too rapidly to talk, smile, or acknowledge another human presence. I kept running from room to room trying to hurry everybody up. Leigh remembered a last-minute phone call. It was close to an hour after dinner. Pete had finished the dishes and boiled water for a pot of tea which he finally brought into the living room on a tray, along with cups, sugar, honey, and spoons. Somehow, we all finally gathered together, sitting on chairs and couches, or stretched out on the floor around the low, circular table in the center of the room.

We began to talk about routine housekeeping matters, our nervousness abating so long as we talked about who was going to fix the leaky bathroom faucet, and which car could be used at the co-op on Thursday. About ten o'clock we took a break and I put Matt to sleep. When I got back downstairs Gary was sitting cross-legged on the floor, his back to the fireplace, shifting nervously.

"I have something I want to talk about, but I don't know if it's appropriate to bring it up," he said, his voice just a bit higher and reedier than usual. My stomach tightened up.

"It's something I want to share about some of the problems Anne and I are dealing with," he continued. He wanted help, it was true; but it was just as true that he had decided to take the first plunge, had decided to take that on as his responsibility.

"Go ahead, Gary," Ruth said, as if the preliminaries were going to drive her up a wall.

"How do you feel about me talking about these things?" he asked Anne.

She was sitting on the rocker, across the circle from Gary, her blue eyes alert. One foot, in a furry house slipper, tapped lightly on the floor. Her small, square, compact hands gripped both arms of the rocker firmly.

"Sure, okay," she said.

There was a pause, while Gary seemed to take a mental deep breath.

"I feel like you're not accepting me the way I am," he finally said in a burst, looking directly at her. "You keep pushing me to change, and I don't understand what it is you want. But I feel like you want me to be something I'm not."

Anne answered rapidly, "The way you look at our relationship it's all about my problems. You make it sound like you don't have any problems of your own, so I wind up feeling like the fucked-up one." Her face was angry. "There's so much you aren't willing to look at. I feel like you're not really open to me and willing to share with me. I'd like us to be closer than we are."

I rolled my neck to loosen the taut muscles and unclenched my jaw. I was gripped by the enormous tension between them. My sympathy was more with Anne, yet that made me feel guilty, made me suspect that I was silently siding with her because she was a woman, rather than because of what she said. Way at the back of my mind there was a flicker of a thought that I wanted to see Gary punished for being so much like me. But more consciously I thought that they were serious, and by having it out at a house meeting they were indicating that they expected something from all of us, from me. I was excruciatingly self-conscious. I had to squelch an impulse to laugh, and another to say, "Oh, this is just a lot of crap." The division between sincerity and the ridiculous is flimsy at times, especially when I am called upon to give more than I am sure I have available. I felt as if I were set down upon a proving grounds.

There were signs of similar recognitions among the other people. Dan stretched, and shook himself loose. Chris looked petrified, eyeballing around. Leigh was leaning forward, her fingers splayed across her thighs.

"What things do you want to share more of Gary asked indulgently.

"Like your family," Anne said, angry but not adamant, as if this ground had all been covered before. "Every time I say anything about how your family might have influenced the way you are, you react like I'm attacking you."

"Look, Anne, I've thought as much about my family as I know how," he said, his voice rising again. "I feel like you're pushing me to admit that I'm fucked up because you want me to feel the way you do about things."

"You see what I mean," Anne yelped, "you always make it that I fucked up. You're not listening to me. Every time I try to talk to you about any of this you get defensive and begin to intellectualize and verbalize and shut me off."

"Why don't you just let me alone then?" Gary shouted in exasperation.

"Because there's more I want from you," Anne shouted back. "I want you to start taking my perceptions seriously. I'm no dummy. I want you to understand that you've got problems, too, just like everybody else."

"For chrissake, Anne . . ." he said, his voice thick with frustration. He turned toward the couch where Pete, Ruth, and I were sitting. "What am I doing wrong'?" he wailed. "I just don't understand." And though I was struck by the theatricality of his question, his bewilderment was so genuine that I softened at once.

"It doesn't sound like you're really hearing Anne," Pete said, encouraged by his ties to both of them. "Yeah . . . she's saying that you're treating her like a patient with a problem. And she's telling you that she feels boxed in by that. I think you're really trying to mold her into the image you have of a woman and a marriage."

"But you know, Anne," I said, "it really does sound as if you're pressing Gary to be what you want him to be, that you're not being patient about his way of working things out." I was aware of wanting to give Gary some support,worried that Anne would get so much sympathy that Gary would feel all alone.

"I know," Anne said. "But I feel so goddamn frustrated I don't know what else to do."

"Why are you taking your frustration out on me? That's what I don't understand," Gary said sullenly.

"It sounds like what you're saying to Anne," Ruth said slowly, concentrating on each thought, "is that you've got everything accounted for, that you understand what you need to. And that really frustrates her because it makes all the problems the two of you have her fault, it makes her feel guilty. It's like you're saying that she should straighten herself out, that it's not your problem. But she's got this enormous investment in you, in your relationship, and that's what's frustrating her. She doesn't want to walk away from your problems, and she doesn't want you to turn your back on them, she wants the two of you to work this out together."

"I don't know," Gary said sadly. "Everybody keeps telling me to look at myself, but I don't know what to look at." What an admission for him to make, staring into his own opaque depths.

"It sounds like you don't believe you've got an unconscious," Chris said, after a long hesitation during which he wondered if what he wanted to say was true, knew that he wanted to contribute something perceptive–the atmosphere of the house meeting seemed to demand nothing less–but feared that his shot in the dark would wound.

But in fact his thought fell like a pebble in the pool of Gary's musing, and set off ripples of meaning and understanding. An unconscious? Precisely what was meant by that? Gary wondered. He was learning that he saw himself differently from the ways the rest of us did. Just when he was being charitable, making an allowance for another one of Anne's damn irrational perversities, Leigh would tell him he was being sanctimonious; at just the moment when he was acknowledging that everything might not be the way he thought it was, Ruth told him he sounded defensive. He couldn't avoid knowing that he was missing the point. He was being told that there were more things he didn't understand than he had imagined, but being told by people whom he trusted–people who seemed to believe in him. He tried as hard as he could to be honest, because he expected that of himself. Now he had to confess that he didn't know as much about himself as he thought he did–a realization which presented itself anew every few years.

We talked on and on, until anxiety gave way to tiredness; tempers still flared but stamina was sapped. Early in the morning all the men were clustered around Gary, while Leigh and Ruth flanked Anne. When Gary and Anne finally went to bed, they were uncertain of where to proceed, of what to do next. But what had happened that night would inform the rest of our lives on Cliveden street. More barriers of privacy had come down than I had anticipated. We had tried to help. Much later I would begin to think that I, and everybody else, had extended more understanding than warmth, that our responses, though animated by sincerity, were inhibited by the caution of our involvement. Still, the impact of what had passed reverberated through our individual experiences. Leigh began to see that there was a difference between the battles she had witnessed in her childhood and the conflict between Gary and Anne Gary and Anne had fought hard, but unlike Leigh's parents they hadn't tried to destroy each other, hadn't hit and hurt each other when words no longer had a capacity to do damage. Chris was put in touch with his own lack of confidence in his perceptions, and Ruth and I, though we didn't talk about it, thought that our time, too, would come. Pete was confirmed in his faith that Gary was a man to admire, that he was rock-like in his willingness to do what he must.

The next morning Gary was in a deep funk, his unhappiness was palpable. Anne, worried that she was pushing too hard, sought reassurance from me and from Leigh, Ruth, and Pete. Soon afterward, Gary went into psychotherapy. Pete worried that a shrink would turn Gary into a jellyfish. But Gary saw no other recourse. He was in up to his neck, and didn't want to chance sinking any lower. After a few weeks Anne went into therapy along with Gary, and despite continued doubts, they both seemed to be more satisfied. But as Gary opened up, as they began to have more fun together, to find their lovemaking more satisfying, to fight without always having a feeling of nagging guilt and resentment afterward, Anne started to worry that she wouldn't be able to handle the responsibility for the deepening of their bond. As Gary began to show her more directly that he loved her and depended on her, she felt unreliable, as if she wouldn't come through for him. But at the same time she couldn't help seeing that so far she had been strong enough for him to lean on her when she had to. With an enormous sense of relief she stopped asking herself if the marriage would survive and began to concentrate instead on ways that she could make it better. Much of what was passing between them transpired when they were alone; they set aside evenings up in their room, nights when they ate dinner out, weekends when they went camping.

By having the courage and trust to make the rest of us privy to the conflict at the heart of their relationship they had opened up a vast, flexible psychic space in which we could all begin to explore what we wanted to get from living in the house. It seemed during that house meeting, and in the weeks immediately afterward, that most of us were ready to accept some responsibility for being available to each other when asked, and when our own lives permitted. I felt more secure about making emotional demands be cause I anticipated that there would be a response. The next few weeks were animated by ceaseless conversation: all over the house, late at night and early on weekend mornings, over breakfast and dinner, we talked in twos and in groups, ever shifting, like cells involved in growth, seeking and giving, learning about one another. I began to think that if I slept at all I would miss something crucial, began to experience a deep, jealous possessiveness about the lives of the people with whom I was living. It was akin to the feeling when a man and a woman discover they have a passion for each other: most everything else is, for awhile, crowded out of the forefront of their consciousness. Except that, because we weren't lovers, the mood was more one of unacted upon incest; the air was thick with longing. The house meetings were the points in time at which feeling coalesced.

A group identity was taking shape. What had happened between Gary and Anne had involved us all, both with them, and within ourselves. We had moved past intentions. Chris' trepidation, Dan's silence, Ruth's earnestness, Gary's faith, Anne's determination were all characteristic, and out of them a group style was coming together. We were consciously supportive of each other, we were even handed, and reluctantly critical. There was just enough tenderness to ease the shock of our group-probe into private realms.

*   *   *

Ruth felt freed-up in the house. Never had she been less resentful of other people, of their presence in her life. Both at home and at work there was a premium placed on people speaking their minds. She began to sense that there was enough acceptance in our group so that no single feeling about another person would close off a friendship, would stand by itself as an assessment or an indictment. Never had she felt less judgemental or less likely to be judged, never more at ease to speak her mind.

She was demanding of the rest of us that we explain ourselves, asking for and giving a great deal of sympathetic analysis. She was electrically charged with a desire for candor. One rainy Saturday afternoon a bunch of us were sitting around the living room talking. More than anybody else, Dan was undergoing the frustration of not having found a comfortable place in the life of the group. He was often the recipient of sudden impatience which seemed to shatter against his friendly, impenetrable surface. Ruth asked him why he wasn't more involved than he seemed.

"I don't spend much time trying to figure out where my reactions come from," he answered. "I just sort of deal with situations in ways that feel good."

Ruth was persistent. "Well, the way you're dealing with me isn't making me feel very good. It's making me feel like it isn't very important to you to know me better, or let me know what you're thinking," she said heatedly.

Dan was confused. He was not accustomed to so much talk, to this emphasis on house meetings and personal poking and prodding. He didn't know what Ruth was after, or what he could give her. "Well, I don't know you very well yet," he said.

"Goddamn it, what the hell does that mean?" she shouted, the dam of her restraint giving way. "What kind of rationalization is that? When are you going to make that change? You can use that as an excuse for just as long as you want, you know."

"I'm sorry," he snapped, barely controlling his anger, bristling with it, "but that's just the way it is." He felt dreadfully cut off, attacked by Ruth, and he suspected that somewhere in her–and in me, and in some of the others was a pain so deep that it made her be cruel. He wanted to say, Keep away from me! He was trying like hell to relax, to make this place his home, but he thought that this was how people destroyed each other, not how they grew together.

He was accustomed to getting close to people by messing and joking around, just sort of bouncing off each other, as you came closer and closer. But people here weren't doing much of anything together except for talking. He felt vastly different, separate. Time and again he would be told by Ruth, or Gary, or Leigh–seemingly growing more sure of herself as she found the rest of us echoing her complaints–that we didn't know what to make of his long, enigmatic smiles. His level, warm gaze seemed to signal so much more than just friendliness, there was hurt and bafflement and longing in it too. But whatever message he wanted to send was not making its way across the silent space bordered by his intensity and Gary's or my perplexity. Dan needed to feel that the group in which he was living was pure, perfect–these qualities would be the source of its strength, would allow it to reach out beyond its confines and touch the lives of other people, would be its political essence. What he wanted from the rest of us was help in building his dream–that, and to be friendly. But it wasn't working out that way and it was painful for him, playing it by ear with so many folks, never being sure of what ground he shared. It wasn't long before he was tied up in the hospital; he had decided to return to medical school and finish his last semester. About his life in the hospital he was by and large uncommunicative. His work there was time consuming and demanding, but also a way to avoid the pain of home.

At the time I was too immersed in the day-to-day details of our life together to notice how our emphasis had shifted from the political orientation of our group meetings the previous spring to the more intimate and personal mood of the first months in the house, and how, in the course of that change, Dan had become alienated. It was as if when we had been trying to imagine what our lives would be like together, our vision–essentially intellectual–had been cast in terms of our beliefs. Now that we were all under one roof, though, there was nothing very much to be said about what we believed–it was obvious that despite differences among us we all hewed to similar political visions. No longer would the rigidity of what we believed be adequate, some more supple and limber knowledge was now available and in demand. Our politics was incorporated into our arrangements: into our money sharing, our departure from traditional sex roles, into the whole notion of communality. Ideology crept out of our conversations, more joking familiarity snuck in.

The weeks rolled into each other. Soon fires were crackling in the living room. Those thick stone walls, natural air conditioning in August, were chill-conductors in October. We were discovering one another. Anne yelled a lot, in a joyful, exuberant way. And when she wanted out of the mass activity, she disappeared into her room and shut the door.

Gary came out of his depression. One Wednesday night he and Dan, playing around in the living room, did a slow-motion dance while they passed a cold, wet ice cube back and forth. Soundless, spinning around the room, while the rest of us sat rapt. They were so beautiful. With a start I remembered that Dan, who had a leonine grace, hadn't danced until he was eighteen years old. Matt and Ruth began a shaving cream fight one night which eventually snared us all, tearing and shrieking up and down staircases brandishing aerosol cans. Pete, still awed by his readjustment, was treading cautiously for fear of stepping in a pile of shit and finding it was his own.

As for Chris, he was stationed at the absolute center of our lives, using the living room as a bedroom, an arrangement that began to rouse some noticeable displeasure. Chris was the only night dweller in the group. By midnight, when most of the rest of us were in bed or on the way there, he was just leaving the house to begin his day's socializing; often his eyes were red-rimmed from lack of sleep. One result of this conflict in timestyles was that Chris would often be out of the house when the rest of us were spending time together, and so he was, like Dan, subtly excluding himself–it wasn't long before some of us began to exclude him as well. In the late morning and sometimes the early afternoon, Chris would be asleep on the couch, effectively shutting off access to the comforts and amenities of the living room. I protested the inconvenience; Gary offered to help Chris get his room ready; Leigh said she didn't want him Hopping in her room the way he had before– she recalled that it had taken six months before Chris was ready to occupy his room in their last house. Ruth suggested that he might be avoiding settling in so that the possibility of flight remained open. And for the first time I came smack up against Chris' stubborn resistance to this kind of group pressure.

"My room isn't ready yet," he said, and it was apparent in the way he said it that he felt cornered. The work he had planned was ambitious and time-consuming, but he had little time to spare. He said he could work comfortably only when there was daylight. What with sleeping late and teaching there was precious little daylight available. The harder anybody pushed Chris, the more he balked.

So, loose ends sailing along behind, Chris would grab a pile of books and papers, dash off to teach a Latin class–a medium-sized guy, with an enormous pile of kinky, tousled hair, wearing a yellow knit shirt with a faded red lobster on the front, always behind schedule, straining against the grain with such pleasantness and kindness that was liked wherever he went.

Ruth thought Chris was kind, considerate, gentle, intelligent, knowledgeable and maddening, absolutely maddening. Her ambivalent feelings made it harder for her to live with him than with anybody else in the house. She felt responsible for him, maternal yet resentful. He went to such great lengths to do her small favors that she felt guilty. His chivalry was remarkable, it was as if he had been born in the wrong century. Ruth would be doing the dishes and Chris would say, "If you don't feel like finishing, leave some for me. I'll get to them when I get home." The next morning the dirty dishes she had left behind would still be piled in the sink, and Ruth would find herself resenting Chris for not having done her work for her. His impulse to be kind exceeded the limits of his real capacity to be helpful.

Leigh, meanwhile, was still spending a night every week or two with a man she had begun to see while Dan was in Colorado during August. Dan said he wasn't hurt or jealous. But a few weeks after he came back to town he met Joan; they were both planning to do their internships at the same hospital. Dan liked her right off–there was something buoyant and physical and good-timey about her, an ease about the way she moved and used her body, a competence, a willingness to exert herself, a friendly laughter which punctuated much of what she said. She seemed vital and uncomplicated, bright but not ponderous. And she wanted to go to bed with Dan. They spent only a brief time together before she returned to Cleveland where she was finishing medical school–but they arranged for her to stay at our house the last weekend in October when we had planned a great communal bash, a gigantic party to celebrate Halloween and the existence of our house.

The night of the party came. All of us were in a nervous tizzy about what the night would be like. Joan and Dan had gone off that morning and weren't back yet. A rock band was setting up in the living room, and its lead guitarist was the man Leigh was seeing. I remember dashing into the kitchen stoned-out paranoid, and saying, "Listen, I've really got to know if you people like me." Pete and Gary both gave me reassuring hugs and then we all laughed and laughed. Around eight, people began to show up . . .

By ten there were about two hundred people massed in the house-many, many more than we had expected. A glut of people streamed through the house, filling every available space and corner; some were in costume and some weren't–with a few of our friends it wasn't always apparent. People tripping and stoned and drunk; sweating, laughing and shouting to be heard. A guy I had long suspected of being a narc accosted me in a hallway wearing drag and with his face painted white. "Hiiiuh, Mike," he trilled. I was so spun out on the paranoia of feeling invaded that I couldn't be sure whether I had imagined him or not. Smiling faces that I almost recognized kept appearing in front of mine, and then being disappeared. The floors were shaking–those solid, seventy-year-old hardwood floors the whole stone house was swaying with the weight of dancing bodies. Matt was asleep in the corner of the living room dressed like a tiger, exhausted by a night of trick or treat. After a while I tried to shut myself away in my room, but my heart was pounding and I felt like a deserter from the front lines of a war I had helped to start because I thought it would be a lark. I edged my way back through a throng of strangers and, seeing a friend, dropped down beside him on the front steps. Two kids–they couldn't have been older than sixteen–were heading out the front door carrying a case of our beer, the last case. I jumped up and yelled and started after them. So did a lot of other people. I ran for a block or so, and then thought, the hell with it. Back inside the eight of us gravitated toward a small clearing in the middle of the dining room. We embraced in a football huddle, arms around each other's shoulders, swaying to the music, hoping to ward off the evil spirits. No luck. The next morning, a gray, damp Sunday, we cleaned up and settled quietly in the living room in front of a fire. We felt close. The Sunday papers were strewn across the floor, and we read or talked desultorily. Late in the afternoon Leigh and Pete ventured out into the gloom and brought home a delicatessen supper.

Home Life

The leaves had all fallen off the trees and empty nests were revealed in the high, bare branches. More and more of our time was being spent indoors, there were fewer opportunities to wander away. At four o'clock on a crisp, sunny Friday afternoon in November Matt and Jono were building a fort in the front hall out of blankets, chairs, rope, bricks, pillows, and eight-year-old fantasies. They entered their stronghold by sliding down the banister and jumping over the railing. I was sitting in the living room tending a tire and reading the third volume of Doris Lessing's Children of Violence. Upstairs, Anne was taking her aftenoon nap, while Chris was whistling out in the kitchen, like the Creator toying with chaos and delight. I didn't know what supper would be, but I knew this much: it would be delicious and it would take all the king's horses and all the king's men to put the kitchen together again.

About five I heard Gary pull into the driveway on his motorcycle. He walked into the house wearing a knit cap under a gold helmet, heavy gloves and two layers of coat. After a stop in the kitchen for peanut butter and jelly and a gulp of milk straight from the gallon container in what Matt called the Cliveden Club style, he headed for the third floor.

Leigh and Pete arrived home about the same time, and both of them checked the mail on the breakfront in the hall before Pete went to his room, closed the door behind him, and played the guitar for an hour. Leigh tromped out to the kitchen, sat down on the red, three-step ladder and began to help Chris slice vegetables. At that point four pots, a frying pan, two bowls, a colander, two spatulas, a wooden mixing spoon, an egg beater, a set of measuring cups, three glasses, a cup, two plates, four teaspoons and three tablespoons, and a half-dozen knives had been brought into play.

Near six Ruth came through the door in a burst of cold air, gave me a kiss, hit the refrigerator for a piece of muenster cheese with mayonnaise and a glass of apple cider, and then went to our room to do yoga. I drove Jono home and when I got back Chris asked me to set the table for dinner; I enlisted Matt's help and we set fourteen places, because we were expecting live guests. Ruth came downstairs and so did Pete and soon our friends arrived. Some people sat down in the living room, others were out in the kitchen drinking sherry and wine–the two groups were fluid, people passed back and forth from room to room. About 7:30 Chris shouted, "Okay, dinner," and we all tiled into the dining room while he ladled out bowls of Hittite soup from a cauldron. While we ate the soup a number of conversations began around the long table, merging into a babble of gentle noise and sudden exclamations. Matt began to tell us about an adventure during which he almost fell from a treetop just as a salad of tomatoes and cucumbers seasoned with dill, mint and lemon arrived at the table.

"This is soooo good," Anne said.

"Do you always eat like this?" a friend asked around a mouthful of salad.

"Only when Chris cooks," Gary and Leigh answered at the same time.

Matt was still up in the tree. When he got back down safely Ruth sighed deeply and said, "I just got twenty seven new gray hairs."

The mood at the table was frantically mellow, the feeling that always seemed to set in at the beginning of a weekend, as if our motors, revved up all week long, were running down toward a slow idle in spurts and dashes.

"Ruth thinks I'm getting more gray hairs," I said.

"No, you're just getting bald," Gary said mischievously.

"Me? Me?" I shouted. "That empty space on your crown must be affecting your eyesight, baby."

Just then everything quieted down for a minute when Chris brought in a foot-long baked salmon cake, shaped to look like a fish; its crust was golden brown, its aroma was tantalizing.

"Too fucking much," Pete said, and took a big swig of beer from his glass.

While we were filling our plates Ruth said, "You know what I heard at work today? If you have dreams about your teeth falling out it expresses castration anxiety."

Pete snorted.

"Who said that?" Anne asked.

"Ruth did," I replied.

"The closest thing that I've had to a nightmare in a long time is dreaming that all my teeth were falling out of my mouth," Leigh said. "Chris, will you put a little more salmon on my plate? It's really delicious."

"Oh, it's nothing," he said elaborately, parodying himself. While he dished out the salmon he said, "I used to dream about catching my penis in my zipper and its falling off." He laughed with embarrassment.

Ouch, I thought, and moved my knees together.

"Chris, that's fairly obvious," Anne exclaimed amid a lot of laughter. "I had a dream this week about a huge man coming after me with a flaming sword and sticking it down my throat."

"Hmmm. What could it mean'?" Ruth mugged.

"Sometimes," Gary said seriously, "A sword is just a sword."

"No dear," Anne said with sarcastic affection, "not this sword."

"God, this is a delicious meal," I mumbled through a mouthful of sweet custard stuff, and took a sip of Turkish coffee.

A few of us helped to clear the table while the others drifted across the hall into the living room. Another log was thrown on the fire. Gary washed the dishes and I put away the leftovers and wiped the dining-room table. Ruth made a pot of tea and brought it inside with a bunch of cups, but a minute later Pete came out to the kitchen, took a cup from the cupboard, and went back to the living room. Months later he told me that he had still been using his own cups because they gave him a symbolic hold on his in dependence. I kept Gary company, and when the kitchen work was done he got his harmonica and we Went inside where Leigh and one of our friends were both strumming guitars. Dan took the tambourine off its peg on the wall, and we all sang for awhile. Matt took the television upstairs to watch a monster movie, and Chris went to watch with him. At about eleven I tucked Matt into bed, assured him that the monster wasn't real and besides it hung out in Japan, and came back downstairs. By one in the morning our friends had all gone home and we were drifting off toward bed. Finally only Leigh and Chris were left in the living room and then only Chris. He got on his coat and drove off in the Toyota and the house was still. In our room Ruth and I built a fire, made love, and fell asleep with our bodies pressed together side by side.

* * *

When I came downstairs Saturday morning Anne was doing her wash in the laundry room behind the kitchen and Dan was in the living room piddling around on a guitar. The house looked like a disaster zone. I made myself a pot of tea, all the while humming loudly and off key, laughing, snorting, shadow boxing. When Anne walked through the kitchen I hesitated, but I was beginning to relax enough around the people I lived with to no longer feel foolish about making public some bits and snatches of my running interior monologue–strange, irrelevant remarks, private observations, dialects, songs, scatology. When my tea was brewed I wandered aimlessly from room to room, and then checked out my house job on the wheel in the dining room. The wheel was two concentric circles made of colored cardboard. The larger, outer circle was divided into eight pie-shaped slices, each marked with one of the adults' names; the inner circle was marked with eight household tasks. Every week we rotated the tasks among us. The jobs included cleaning the kitchen, the three bathrooms, the living and dining rooms, doing a supermarket shop, picking up the co-op order, cleaning all the halls, and looking after the yards and back rooms. By noontime Saturday most of us were at work.

The decision to divide the housework in this fashion–making no distinction between men's work and women's work–was based on the belief that men and women are both unnecessarily limited by their usual sex roles. Either role can be the source of endless tension and wear if it doesn't suit an individual. Certainly there are profound differences between men and women. But I don't think that women are better suited to wash the dishes or cook the meals, to do all the mindless but necessary work, to settle for domestic satisfactions alone. Nor are men all cut out for batterings of the marketplace. I think the movement toward Communality in the lives of most of the people in the house grew out of wanting to bring our political values closer to home. I knew that the foundations of the state wouldn't shudder because we all took our turns washing the toilets–or, for that matter, because we shared half our incomes. Nor did I think that the way to change our country was for everybody to move into communes and put wheels on the wall. But for us, our desire to escape sex role stereotyping in our home was something we could accomplish without twisting ourselves out of shape. Starting fresh with a form of living arrangement that was experimental, we had the freedom to create it in ways that pleased us and nurtured our growth.

Our arrangements are all of a piece, all interwoven: money sharing, readjusting sex roles, holding house meetings, demanding communal responsibility of one another. They are the fabric out of which we are fashioning a tiny sub-society which values productive, independent, non-harmful work, caring and being cared for, warmth and spontaneity. If we want it badly enough, and if we are strong and diligent, our dissatisfaction may someday mature into a true community, part of the larger society and yet with its own way of living, working, raising children.

Dan says that living in a group gives him an identity and a security he would otherwise lack. "It's almost like we're no different from ancient men who went around in tribes," he told me. "We have this big fucking world that we don't have any idea how to deal with by ourselves, and we feel insecure and hopeless at all the stupidity and cruelty in it. But somehow we feel strength in groups of people. On one level or another all the people in our house have the same gut feeling that we just need to hang together with other people."

*   *   *

It was soon apparent in our group that our inclinations toward housework and tidiness varied all right, but not according to sex. Gary, Anne, and I were the neatest and fussiest; Ruth and Chris had the most difficulty keeping things neat or doing their house jobs. But there were areas of special individual concern. Dan, for instance, would usually go out of his way to clean up a mess in the kitchen or the front yard; I hated to clean the halls but looked after the fireplaces; Chris, though sending him into the bath rooms was akin to condemning him to the lion's den, did more than his share of cooking and put in long hours caring for the yard and garden.

The question of how neat and clean our house should be remained contentious and frustrating throughout the year; Chris, especially, was isolated by it again and again. But when we began to talk about neatness we very soon found ourselves led into the issue of responsibility in a commune. In what ways were we obligated to each other? How were we to set and enforce standards? How did we deal with nonconformists in our midst? I agreed with Pete when he said, "You've got to put more into a system than you take out of it to keep the system going." But the way we lived was unorthodox, and so we had cut ourselves off from a lot of useful traditional notions about responsibility in the life of a family. Some of the kinds of frustration and dis pleasure arising from our peculiar rootlessness were expressed at a house meeting early in the winter.

After a long, nervous silence I told Chris that I felt smothered and annoyed by him. "Whenever I'm critical of you, the way you react makes me feel like I'm on the verge of destroying you," I said sharply, but still holding back the full force of my anger. "Sometimes I say things to you that I think are pretty innocuous, but you react defensively, and So I feel constrained and I begin to collect injustices rather than express them on the spot."

"I don't feel that you're justified in feeling resentful," Chris said, retreating before the potential explosiveness of my anger. As he shrank back the sensation was familiar to him–it reminded him of how he felt when as a kid playing by himself he would run to hide behind a tree when he heard somebody approaching. The terrain had changed, but the sensation had not. "You haven't tested out my reactions by talking to me," he said. "And I'd need some examples to know what you're talking about."

I was sure that he did know what I was talking about. "Okay," I said, struggling to be reasonable, "like last week you were cooking and I asked you what time dinner would be ready. And instead of answering my question you laid out all sort of rationalizations and justifications for its being late. All I wanted to know was *when* I'd be eating so I could make my plans for the evening. But your reaction told me that by asking I was putting you uptight. Now the next time I may not ask you because it's too much of a hassle, and so I'll probably feel resentful for being inconvenienced. That kind of situation. seems to happen again and again." I knew I sounded pedantic.

"That's a bad example," Chris said defensively. "I'm more likely to say, 'When the eggplant is ready,' than to give you the time. And if you're the fifth person to ask me, then that will put me uptight."

"Well, Jesus, I have no way of knowing all that," I snapped. Goddammit, I didn't want to bog down in Chris' bottomless pool of rational and absurd arguments, I wanted to get to the source of the tension, not muck around in our mutual resentment and defensiveness.

"I know you've been mad at me," he said, struggling to put the exchange on a more equal footing.

"I'm not saying that I'm mad at you," I answered crossly. His frightened look, his voice catching and growing higher and softer–something weak about his style of defending himself–made me Want to just swat aside his objections; and that angry impulse in the face of his seeming fright made me feel like a bully. I was sullen.

"That's how it appears to me," Chris said. "It's hard for me to say what's annoying to me because I feel like I complain all the time, and about such stupid things."

"That blows my mind," Anne interjected. "I never hear you complain about anything."

"Maybe you're complaining," Ruth said quietly, "but just keeping it to yourself, not saying it out loud."

"You know," Gary said, "it's reasonable for you and I to have a relationship and part of it to be feeling and expressing anger. Harmony isn't the same as a relationship. If I end up having to walk on eggshells with you, and it builds up in my head, then I'm going to end up feeling smothered, which is what Mike is talking about."

To Chris, Gary sounded instructive, perhaps even condescending. He didn't know how to reply so he said nothing and there was a silence during which people stirred, shifted position. Dan sat up from where he had been stretched out on the floor and filled a cup with tea.

"Sometimes, Chris, I get the feeling that you think that you're basically a shit because you're not neat," Leigh said in an exploratory, protective way. "I feel as though you think these trivial things go way down to some gut feelings of inadequacy about yourself."

"Amen," Ruth murmured.

"I've been told I'm sloppy all my life," Chris said to Leigh. He seemed to find it easier to respond to her than to Gary or me; from the time she had brought him into the group, Leigh had protected Chris. "I sometimes feel as though lines are drawn and I don't have any say in where they're drawn," he said forlornly. "I feel that if I said the living room is so neat

66

and clean that it feels sterile, my feeling would be put down as inconsequential."

Anne said, "You know, when I visited your home I got the feeling it would be pretty hard to grow up in a house as neat as that and not have some pretty strong feelings about neatness, one way or another."

"My mother's reason for being neat was always what other people would think," Chris answered. "And I didn't think that was a good reason for doing anything."

"It seems like you feel a lot of rebellion when people talk about neatness," Ruth suggested.

I had worried that the meeting might turn on my bullying of Chris. So I was relieved to hear that my complaints were understood and partially echoed by Gary, by Anne, by Ruth, and even by Leigh. Their agreement made me even more impatient to have done with it.

"You get all tangled up in intellectual trips about neatness," I said in a clotted voice. "But what I want is for you to try and respond to me and what I need and not to your mother's reasons for doing things." I wanted Chris to change on the spot, and I was too angry to make any allowance for what he wanted.

"I respond," he said sharply, fed up with my abrasiveness. "I'm just not good at cleaning up and everybody knows that."

"Well, fuck that," I shouted. "Grow up! What the hell does that mean, 'I'm not good at cleaning up.' You're a grownup, Chris. You've got to come to grips with the standards of the people you're living with."

God, it felt good to blow my cork.

"When I do try to clean up, I find that I've done it all wrong," he said. It seemed to him that the more he defended himself the angrier I got. Then, for the first time, it occurred to him that it might be his way of defending himself which made me angry at him. But caught in the midst of the argument he didn't have the time or calm to think more about it.

"I really sympathize with that, Chris," Ruth said, with enough vehemence for me to understand that she was trying to help Chris fight back against me, that she allied herself with his predicament under my onslaught. "When I try to clean up I feel as though I walk a mile moving stuff without making any headway. And I find it very hard to ask for help."

"I think, Chris," I said more calmly, "that what I'm trying to get at is that you don't take responsibility for yourself."

"On a basic level," Gary said pompously, "I think each of us here accepts the others as individuals. And I think that situation affords us a unique opportunity to test out the things we're afraid of. The opportunity is here, Chris, for you to say if you're uncomfortable or pissed off about something. When something upsets you, open your mouth. An opportunity like this doesn't come along very often. As for me, I'm going to make a greater effort to tell you what I'm feeling right on the spot, no matter how worried I am about how you'll receive it. That.seems to me to be my responsibility."

Very obliquely Gary had hit on a home truth about Chris: he never complained until somebody complained about him, and then he responded by counterattacking.

"The problem isn't just in Chris testing it out, but in the rest of us testing it out, too," Leigh agreed with Gary.

"What are you feeling about Chris right now?" Pete asked me.

"Well, I don't think I can say what Gary and Leigh did," I said, responding to what I sensed was a group pressure for me to adopt their more sympathetic attitudes. "I think it's a right thing to say, but I just don't feel resolved enough about the tensions between us, or about Chris' willingness to really act on all of this. I couldn't commit myself to the kind of effort Gary did."

"Chris, you have a responsibility to consider how people feel about you," Anne said persuasively. "And you also have a responsibility to let us know how you feel about us, and about what demands are made on you living the way we do. You owe it to us to let us know what your reactions are. That's part of our agreement. And I think it's what Mike is talking about when he talks about responsibility."

"Well," Chris said, "I don't think that people are letting out their feelings to me on the spot, the way they want me to."

"That's true," Anne said.

"Mike, I feel as though you have some awful, concrete things to say to me that you haven't said," Chris told me.

"No," I replied.

"You know, I think the two of you are playing a cat and mouse game," Leigh said shortly. "I think you've got to be willing to move, too, Mike, or you can't expect that Chris will."

*   *   *

Each night, everybody who was home sat down together for a family-style supper. Most of us had meetings and other commitments which took us out of the house several evenings each week–Anne went to her consciousness raising group and Leigh to hers, and to a women's health collective as well; Chris went folk dancing and sometimes to Gay Activist Alliance coffee hours; Gary attended community meetings related to his work and had shrink appointments; Pete was organizing a nutrition course and was frequently out on dates. Only Ruth and Dan were usually home at night when the year began, but all of us spent more evenings at home, by chance and design, as the year progressed. Usually, we would all eat as a group a few times a week, and on Mondays, before house meetings, we always gathered around the dining-room table, chattering through supper with nervous, affectionate anticipation.

We all took turns cooking. When you wanted to cook you signed up in advance on a calendar posted on the refrigerator door, and you handled dishwashing the same way. We rotated the cooking among us by deciding that everybody was responsible for preparing supper about every eighth day. The system was flexible enough so that you could cook pretty much when you wanted to. Nobody ever shirked either cooking or dishwashing; I don't really know why, except that maybe we were growing to care for each other in so many more involving and important ways that these simple tasks which made our lives more orderly and pleasant seemed to reflect our commitment. Every two or three weeks we'd decide on the spur of the moment to go out for ribs or pizza. Otherwise, though, a meal was always on the table by seven.

With the exceptions of Gary and Pete we were all experienced cooks. Looking pale and agitated, Gary marched into the kitchen near the end of our first week in the house, made a great commotion, and a few hours later a tuna salad, some porkchops, baked potatoes, corn on the cob, and bread and butter emerged as dinner. Throughout the meal Gary sped back and forth from the dining room to the kitchen, bringing something new on each trip. I thought it was all very funny and kept laughing at the expressions on his face, but everybody else hushed me. A few months later Gary made mushroom crepes for dinner.

Pete's earliest meals were precise and delicious–I never would have guessed that he had seldom cooked for himself when he lived alone. During the year he developed an interest in nutrition; his cooking came more and more to reflect his concern, and then began to influence the rest of us as well. Gary began to eat vegetables and to enjoy cooking them, and by May I had become a vegetarian. Matt voluntarily gave up white bread, we stopped buying cookies at the market, We used only fresh vegetables, bought a lot more organically grown food–but we also enjoyed orgiastic relapses of Ginoburgers and Baskin-Robbins sundaes. I felt healthier and virtuous as well. Pete's meals would often have an Oriental flavor, dishes like fried rice and vegetables sauteed in soy sauce. Anne cooked chops and lasagna; Ruth would cook spaghetti with white clam sauce or chicken; I made eggplant parmesan or zucchini and mushrooms. Dan whipped up huge cauldrons of chili, and Leigh made Japanese dishes like sushi. Matt loved to cook, too, and once in awhile, when he was in the .mood and got some help, he'd make sloppy joes or scrambled eggs with ham and mushrooms. He also baked cakes and buns, starting with just raw materials and shunning packaged mixes.

The kitchen, in fact, was the hub of our family life. We had a small table and four chairs in the middle of the room, and there always seemed to be a conversation or a snack or both going on there. A friend said that she could sit in our kitchen on a Sunday morning from eight until noon and have a continuous breakfast with company. In the evenings, too, the kitchen was a gathering place. People coming home from work usually made at least a brief stop there, and on different evenings one or another of us would usually hang around, keeping the cook company, helping out, making the salad which we ate most nights, or just kibitzing.

The kitchen was also where news, gossip, messages and the day-to-day events in our lives were most often exchanged. "I like to sit in the kitchen before supper," Leigh said, "and get the news of the day."

The living room was where we entertained–ourselves and our friends and visitors–but the kitchen was more often where we lived, and where the visitors to our house who were really comfortable hung out, too.

* * *

And where was Matt, the only child in our tribe, throughout those first few months? Well, he was whistling and chirping in the shower on a Sunday night while we sat listening, or smack in the middle of a house meeting asking for an allowance.

Many times his activities would dominate our group life; we would interrupt ourselves for him, or plan an activity; with him in mind. The kind of attention and concern for his welfare–and mine and Ruth's as well–which resulted in there always being somebody to stay home and look after Matt when we were going out was a comfort. We didn't have to hire a babysitter the whole year. But I also worried that living with so many adults was a source of confusion and upset for him.

Ruth was always mindful of being Matt's mother especially when she was doing something unconventional like taking part in political actions or using drugs. She always wondered how her lack of orthodoxy would effect Matt. She

71

found that sharing day-to-day responsibility for him was a relief, but she didn't want her authority to decide what was right and wrong for him to be undermined. It was apparent, for instance, that Dan and Leigh both thought that she was too protective, and their opinions gave rise to a conflict in Ruth: on the one hand she believed Matt should be free to find out for himself what he could handle and what he couldn't, but on the other hand she knew he was just a kid who wasn't yet able to sort out all the complicated events in the adult world around him.

My conflicts were similar. Once, Matt went tearing down the front steps and took a spill on the driveway; a moment later he was back inside bawling his head off. By the time I reached him Gary and Anne were already there, examining his bruise and reassuring him. I saw that he wasn't seriously hurt, gave him a pat on the head and some reassuring words, and went back to what I was doing. I was relieved that even though I was his father I didn't have to act that role at that moment when my mind was elsewhere: I love Matt but I don't always love being a father. But at the same time I thought that as his father my sympathy might have had a special, more significant quality for him. Perhaps, I thought, it will make Matt a less dependent, more resourceful adult having learned to rely upon and trust so many grownups. Or would he resent me for not having provided him a quieter, less complicated harbor? Generally, the question I faced raising Matt in a commune was how and when to share responsibility for him without letting him feel he was deserted by me. The cutting edge of my guilt was blunted by the trust I developed for the other adults in the house. At first it was hard for me to accept when other people disciplined Matt, hard for me to let them supervise him without butting in. But as I watched the adults, one at a time, grow to love him, it became easier.

From the first day in the house Dan was like a big brother to Matt. Ruth loved to watch them play like two kids, Dan goading and leading Matt toward becoming more adventurous, more willing to extend and test the capacities of his line, small, growing body. And she took pleasure in Matt's unabashed admiration for Dan.

Matt was getting the same wonderful confirmation that the rest of us were by living together, the same marvelously increased awareness of the many different ways there are to see and deal with the world, the same daily relearning that one's understanding is never complete and may be questioned and thus increased, the same feeling of inclusion and caring, and the very special attention that came from being the only child in a household with eight adults. But as the only child he sometimes experienced an intense pressure to be adult.

By the winter I had accumulated many images of Matt and the grownups which delighted me. Dan and Matt tearing through the house, Matt screaming in mock/real terror at the game of monster tag. Or Leigh, who said that Matt was so snuggly in the morning, picking him up with his bed blankets and all and dumping him on the floor to start the school day, and then the two of them wrestling and laughing on Matt's floor in the sleepy-headed morning time. "Leigh is really kiddish," Matt said happily. "She really likes messing around. Dan's the same way, he's really nice the way he'll let me stay up until one in the morning or teach me karate." Matt told me that he found it easiest to be punished by Dan and by me. Maybe that's because we're the most unambiguous about setting our limits, but also pretty cajolable within them.

One morning Matt was griping to me about Gary and Anne. "They're always acting like they're my parents," he said. "Like Anne this morning told me to brush my hair." He began to call Gary the Boss in a teasing way which was deadly accurate and fun for them both as well.

I didn't try to pretend that I was less Matt's father because there were other adults sharing his home, and, even if I had, I could hardly have fooled him. Time and again Pete or Leigh or Anne would notice how much more deeply he would sulk if Ruth or I got mad at him, how much more quickly he would bounce back when it was somebody else yelling. But I saw in the tender, fun-filled way that Leigh read him a bedtime story, or the happy light that spread over Pete's face when Matt teased him into playing hockey, or Dan's nonchalance about picking him up and throwing him in the air when Matt asked, "Wanna rassle?" that they were getting as much happiness as they were giving.

The other adults have all had to work out their own ways of dealing directly with Matt, as well as consulting us. Anne got along well with him from the start. So she was hurt when she returned from a winter trip to California and he rushed by her, slowing down for a halfhearted hug only when she hailed him. A while later they sat down in her bedroom for a big powwow, and Matt told her he had been angry at her for not paying enough attention to him. Anne told Matt that she was unhappy at how unresponsive he could be when she hugged him. "I like to really be hugged back when I give somebody a hug," she explained. After a while Matt let her know that she could improve the situation by taking a bike ride with him. And the two of them invented the game of Hugging Monster. "When she catches me," he explained, "she hugs me really tight."

But nothing in our communal life made me feel more alone than being a parent among a group of childless adults. By this time we were talking about Matt almost every week during the house meeting–trying to agree on what rules to set and how to enforce them, and trying to stay informed about his life. We were also beginning to recognize how important it was that we establish clearcut limits and responsibilities for him, and be consistent about enforcing them. But Ruth and I had only each other for empathy, and in that respect we were dissatisfied with our living situation. I felt the distinction acutely during an incident which involved our next-door neighbor, Dave.

Matt, who was the only white kid on the block, was having some problems getting along, and Dave, a black man, told Pete that he thought he could be helpful and wanted to know if he could come over and talk to us all. I had gotten the impression that Dave and his wife disapproved of the way we were raising Matt, and so didn't trust the authenticity of his concern. We talked it over at a house meeting.

"I sense a real difference in attitude in the rest of you," I said. "There's a lot less vulnerability and a lot more curiosity about what Dave has to say. But I'm going to receive what he says about Matt in my guts. It's not going to be some kind of interesting discussion."

"It's been difficult enough to hear from you people about how I'm raising Matt," Ruth added vehemently. "It's also been very worthwhile, but that's because I really trust that you all care about me and about Matt. But I don't trust Dave that way and I don't want to look at everything that everybody in God's creation wants me to."

"It sounds like you're both doing a lot of checking out," Pete said. "I feel like you're cushioning yourselves, maybe excessively."

"Mike and I are checking out whether the rest of you are going to throw your lot in with us," Ruth explained.

"I guess with you, Pete, and with Dan, especially," I added, "I get the feeling that you want Dave to come over so he can be critical of some of Matt's insensitivity to some of the other kids. But I don't think that either of you has been sufficiently sensitive to the fact that Matt has gone to integrated schools all his life, that he's living in a black neighborhood–that he's been exposed to black kids far more than any of us were as kids, and at times it's been difficult for him and he's had reason to be afraid."

In the end, we didn't ask Dave over. And by the spring there was a general recognition that we had to have other children and other parents in our group.

*   *   *

As the days began to shorten and the house was less filled with light we decided to paint the kitchen a bright yellow. During the summer and fall the kitchen had been an airy passage toward the backyard; now it became a bright, warm oasis in the gray days and pitch black nights of winter. As the air became chilly, and more and more time was spent indoors in close quarters, we began to assess our reactions to living together. We were still almost euphorically excited. Sitting around the kitchen table one night Leigh said that she had been spending less time out at meetings.

"I want to spend more time at home with you people," she said, laughing, and then paused thoughtfully. "I guess I think a lot of my running around and activity came from frantically proving my autonomy from Dan. The house has really helped me to see that I'm independent, and I'm feeling less need to prove it." She laughed again. "I developing into a homebody."

"I find that I'm making a lot more decisions now based on how I want to act, too," Chris said. "I was brought up to believe that you never should do anything just for yourself. But every time I've heard one of you people say, 'I did it because I wanted to,' it made me see that I was justified in feeling that way too."

"Incredible," Gary exclaimed.

"You know," Anne said, "my concept of myself as a private person is changing. I miss reading as much as I used to, and making up my own ballet dances in the living room— I'm too self-conscious to do that here, it's not private enough— but I know you people really like me, and that surprises me and gives me the feeling of being okay."

"Who says we like you?" I asked teasingly.

Anne looked hurt but laughed and didn't say anything. She never felt able to tell me when my joking, assertive way had hurt her.

"I think the warmest feeling of belonging I've gotten," Gary said animatedly, "was when we called from L.A. about our flight back and found that you all had already arranged to meet us at the airport. It made me feel like I was coming home."

Though our feelings about ourselves were cozy, though we were settling into a life which felt to us to be not only comfortable but respectable, we learned time and again that it was sometimes hard for the world out there to in corporate us into their versions of reality. Anne, for instance, had been assured by a salesman for Esso heating oil that he would not implement a contract he had persuaded her to sign until she called him back after checking it out at a house meeting. But the next thing she knew an Esso truck pulled up and filled our heater. We reacted by sending an irate letter to the company. It threatened every sort of retaliatory legal mayhem and climaxed with the admonition: You should be ashamed of yourselves! We all signed it. Dr. Peter Kurst signed it. Dr. Gary Rosen signed it. Everybody. Even Gussie Weiss, H.P. (House Pet). I wondered what they made out of such a bizarre communication in the corporate bowels along Esso Road in Bala Cynwyd.

A week later we got an apologetic reply, promising a full investigation and assuring us that Esso had never, ever engaged in deceptive sales practices. Next a company representative, a middle-aged man with a ruddy Wasp face and a neat gray suit, came knocking at our door about 4:30 one afternoon.

The first thing that happened to this guy, who was moving carefully, almost fastidiously, was that Pete started bitching about some tires he had bought from Esso three years ago, and the guarantee, see, the guarantee, was never honored. Buncha crooks. What a scene it must have been from the Esso man's perspective. Red-headed guy with a beard, dressed in a bathrobe mouthing off. Dr. Kurst, yes, hmm, of course. When he was about spouted out, this other geek over there with the ragged cutoffs–his balls would be hanging out except he's got on red silk underpants, can you believe this?–is raving and ranting about pipelines across Alaska and the fucking permafrost. What the fuck has this got to do with heating oil? Just then another one–god, there's a lot of them–he looks like Jesus, this kid, Dr. Yoder I presume, brings in a pot of tea and cups. Christ, I wonder if the cups are clean with the girls sitting here in the living room bitching while Jesus is out in the kitchen whipping up a pot of tea. Oh Christ, it doesn't smell like tea, do you suppose . . . ?

We wrote a second letter.

Dear Esso, Your man Bill H------ is a decent fellow. Thanks for sending him around, we enjoyed talking with him. But your company is still exploiting people, and lying, and destroying the earth, air and water all over the globe and we don't want any of your fucking heating oil. Yours very truly, the Cliveden House Club.

Money Is Honey

Leigh came into my room one winter afternoon and asked me if I wanted a job with Health Information Project helping to put out a monthly newspaper. A job! God, did I ever. Several weeks earlier, immobilized by fear at my inactivity, I had gone into therapy. I hurried down the next day and talked to the other people involved and by the following week I was working half-time on *Philadelphia Health News* and bringing home a cool thirty-five dollars a week, less than what I had earned in a day at the *Evening Sun*. But the job suited me–it gave me time to write, it was my first experience in a collective work situation, it was politically meaningful work, and having an income, no matter how minuscule, meant that I was contributing to the house fund and to my own support. I was satisfied for the time being, and grateful to Leigh. I felt productive and independent in ways which I had begun to miss painfully.

Our house finances were rolling along smoothly and my income wasn't really needed. But our individual doubts about income sharing weren't ameliorated, by any means. When it had been time for Anne to put her first check into the house bank account she had had to contend with her best and her worst instincts, and with deciding which were which. It was her money, she told herself–she had worked hard for it, and she deserved it, every penny of it, and more. Why *should* she give any of it away? At that moment she hadn't really known why, but in went the check nevertheless. And Leigh was still concerned that because she earned so little she would become too dependent on the rest of us, too beholden, that she would undercut the arduously won ground of her own independence. Other people earning little or no money didn't bother her nearly as much as the possibility that she couldn't pull her own weight.

We had figured out that our individual net incomes for the year were probably going to total about $36,000, so that the house would take in about $18,000 all told. That meant that there was about $2,000 to spend on each of us for food, rent, utilities, transportation, household maintenance, and luxuries like going as a group to a restaurant or a movie. That broke down to about $165 per month for most of what was necessary for any one of us to live well, except for clothing and medical expenses, and having Gary and Dan in the house kept our medical expenses low.

We seldom talked about budgeting our housefund, beyond agreeing in general that we wanted to keep our expenses within our means (it was evident that our consciousness of money was formed among the comfortable middle class) and to contribute some money to a ghetto clinic and the city women's center. Each month we spent about $225 for food– that's less than one dollar per day for each person, and our savings at the food co-op and through bulk buying enabled us to shop for and eat most of what we wanted. Rent cost $400; about $150 went for utilities and heat; another $200 on auto insurance and upkeep and other transportation; $150 on household expenses and miscellaneous items (the veterinarian, magazine subscriptions, a new kettle, and so on), and $25 on Matt's school.

* * *

Our first money crisis came when Anne spent sixty dollars of her own money–not house money–on a checked winter coat with a Sherlock Holmes collar. Her purchase set off a buzzing on the house party line because it revealed a flaw in our financial arrangements. Despite equalizing fifty percent of our financial lives, we had left ourselves half–free to live in whatever styles suited us individually. Pete could afford a motorcycle, a ten-speed bicycle, a new suede coat, an Alpine tent, an expensive backpack, a movie camera–all purchases beyond my means. Gary and Anne–now earning nearly twenty-five thousand dollars–had more money for their private use than Leigh, Dan, Chris and I earned altogether. But it was precisely because of the size of their incomes that the rest of us in the house were living so well. On our own, neither Chris, nor Dan, nor Leigh (nor I, except that I shared Ruth's income) could afford a bagels and lox Sunday breakfast, a new record every few weeks, ample supplies of booze and grass, and four cord of firewood–all luxuries which money sharing was making available. It wasn't surprising, in light of these substantial differences, that we thought differently about how to manage our shared money. Nowhere was this more evident than in what we brought home from the supermarket when it was our turn to shop. Dan or Leigh might spend twenty-five dollars, buying just exactly what was needed, perhaps allowing themselves a single, stingy indulgence; Chris or I might spend ten dollars more, bringing home for the extra money some greater portion of necessities and, in addition, a generous helping of olives, ice cream, anchovies or all three; Anne would go to the Germantown Farmer's Market and spend extra money for a higher quality of butter, cheese, eggs, or meat–and even so, she was being more economical than when she and Gary had lived alone; Ruth would spend more money than anybody else at the market, buying kosher dills, bread and butter pickles, and sweet baby gherkins when she was unable to choose among them.

There were two different kinds of problems confronting us. First was the management of the money we agreed belonged to all of us mutually–house money. The second was how we felt about each other's individual lifestyles, and that was still too sensitive for us to talk about openly and fully. In fact, whenever the subject of money came up, our conversations were characterized by defensiveness, self righteousness, inexperience with money sharing, and the fear of having to relinquish one's most cherished comforts and pleasures for the sake of group amity. And there was a great fear of appearing greedy. But Anne's coat, because it cost so much more than some of us could possibly spend on clothing, did finally make these questions and discontents apparent and unavoidable. We were ready to open up the issue of money values, however circumspectly.

Leigh spoke up first, both because of the heat of her feelings and because she had been shopping with Anne when the coat was bought and didn't disapprove of the purchase. She didn't want the discussion to begin with Anne being put on the defensive, and was especially afraid that either Dan or I might do just that.

"In some ways I feel uncomfortable about the money around the house," she said. "It has the potential to screw up my values. I've never had more than I needed before and now I'm beginning to get a sense of non-necessity. I've felt pressure to relate more closely to material needs than I want to. I think we have different attitudes toward money and possessions and don't struggle with that problem very well," she finished, seeming agitated.

"A lot of what makes me uncomfortable around here has to do with how I experienced things when I was growing up," said Dan, speaking up uncharacteristically soon. "People who don't have a lot of money have a very strong consciousness of people who do. The people I grew up with were all people who worked pretty hard and had a sense of how much labor went into growing food or putting a roof over your head, or clothes on your back. There was a real consciousness that people who had a lot of money and a lot of things weren't coming by it by their own labor, it was being accumulated by ways that normal people didn't have access to. Even now when I see my parents accumulating more things–the swimming pool, the house trailer, the boat–I know that my dad has turned into a businessman he's got other people working for him, doing the work he once did.

"People here need to understand," he continued, speaking slowly but decisively, "that when I respond to some body buying a lobster or going to a restaurant it's because I'm getting this jarring feeling inside me, like, where am I and what's going on?"

"You know, my parents couldn't afford a house like this," Chris said, "so I felt kind of funny when my father visited."

There was an undercurrent of competition between Chris and Dan over whose rural background had been more authentic. Dan resented Chris, whom he regarded as an urban dilettante with a taste for fancy foods and foreign movies, laying claim to any of the simple, rural heritage he insisted was uniquely his among our group. Chris thought that Dan exaggerated, substituted bucolic fantasies for facts, and tried to deprive him of his legitimate claim to his own past.

"I was brought up to think of working-class-non working-class distinctions," Chris continued evenly, "but that seems to have broken down in this country. And I was brought up to think that you should never buy anything you can do for yourself, so when I see people buying cookies or granola I think, shit, you should either make it yourself or do without it."

"I think the Mennonite tradition is important to the way I was brought up, too," Dan said right away, as though what Chris had said was no more than a pause in his thought. "Like I've never, ever wanted to be in the position of having to look at myself like the rich man in the story of Lazarus, but now I've sort of got to."

Here was Chris, who was as extravagant as anybody in the house when the mood was upon him, complaining about breakfast cereal. And Dan, who would soon be a doctor, saying that our makeshift, two-thousand-dollars-a-person economy made him feel too rich.

"I think I feel okay when I really sit down and think about something before I buy it," Leigh said, trying to make the discussion more coherent. "What bothers me is that we all know the house has a lot of money and so we stop being conscious of how much we're spending."

"But a lot of what we're able to do financially comes from the fact that we are sharing," Chris said. "I've made less this year than last year, but I've saved more."

"I think," Anne said, speaking up for the first time, and finally setting us on course toward that coat, "that there's group disapproval not of expenditures per se, but it depends on what the money is spent on. Records, dope, bikes, camping equipment, movies are okay. Clothes aren't. The coat incident stands out in my mind. There was a lot of muttering about it, but except for two pairs of sweat socks I haven't bought anything else this year."

"Listen," Ruth said, "Sixty dollars is a reasonable amount for a good winter coat, and I don't think you should have to take any horseshit for it."

"I agree," Leigh said.

"So do I," Chris added. "Besides, it's a really nice coat."

"I want to say how it strikes me," I said, wanting to say something precise and articulate about money values. "I think the decision to share half our incomes was probably harder for the people with larger incomes; after all, it was pretty easy for me to share half of nothing. But there are still disparities in the fifty percent we left ourselves. The reason I've been able to make decisions about what I would do with my life of the kind I've made over the last few years was because first Ruth and now all of you have, in effect, supported me." I was getting bogged down in preface. "But I still feel some jealousy and resentment at the amount of money that Gary and Anne and Pete have to spend on themselves. The coat reminded me of all that. I don't disapprove of the expenditure, but I selfishly want every body else to be forced to live at my income level–and yet I don't want to live on as small an income as Chris'. I don't know," I ended lamely. Ah well, maybe I'd do better next house meeting.

"We have a huge amount of waste and spoilage," Chris said, and once again we veered off on a new course. Never had I heard all of us so reluctant or unable to identify what was troubling us. "We're not conscious," he continued, "of which brand is the cheapest, or maybe we'll get three or four kinds of jams and jellies at one time, and one of them will spoil before we can even finish it. When I go into the kitchen to have a piece of bread I can have plain peanut butter, crunchy peanut butter, peanut butter and honey spread, apple butter, mint jelly, farmer's market butter..." he paused, the list incomplete.

"Margarine," Anne said.

"Strawberry jam, blueberry preserves," I laughed.

"Apricot preserves," Gary added gleefully.

"Grape jelly," Chris said. When we stopped laughing he added. "It gives me the uneasy feeling that we're creating false needs."

It was true, we were wasteful. But the ecological savings involved in living communally were also considerable. Nine people were refrigerators and one stove–and we were learning from each other. Chris taught us to eliminate paper towels, Anne made sure we used phosphate-free detergent. There were probably a dozen other small savings, no one of which was remarkable. But living cooperatively meant that one person's concern, if it was persuasive, communicated itself in action in nine lives.

The conversation meandered for awhile, and then Leigh said, "I need some group pressure to develop a sensible, non-wasteful lifestyle within my means. I feel a need to be pushed in those areas, and that's lacking here."

I thought what she said came closer to the heart of the matter than anything else: we hadn't committed ourselves to the kind of lifestyle Leigh described, and so we were loath to intrude upon each other's privacy by commenting directly on how other people spent their money.

"For the rest of my life," Anne said angrily, "I'm going to be faced with this kind of conflict. Because, goddamm it, I've taught for ten years and I'm going to be well-paid. I'm not going to volunteer, that's just what they'd like women to do. I'm going to have that money and so I'm going to be comfortable."

And, indeed, Anne was accustomed to comfort. And yet, for her, despite having had a family maid and as many cashmeres as any other girl in her high school, political awareness began to grow when she understood that her parents' big house and all their money really weren't making them happy. Contrast that to Dan, whose mother sometimes didn't eat because there wasn't enough for everybody. Or to Pete, whose father made his living as a truck driver, a minimally acceptable job for a Jewish man.

Yet, regardless of these differences in our backgrounds, we had all somehow become members of the same class—our educations had equipped us to earn a living without engaging in either physical labor or commercial enterprise. And it was safe to say, too, that though our disagreements were real and substantial, we were all most concerned that our accommodations with our own materialism be conscious, be within our control. Though Dan believed that poor was virtuous, that labor of the hands was more respectable than labor of the mind; though I was raised to view bosses and Republicans as my enemies; though Ruth and Gary had both been taught that, ultimately, comfort was to be expected; though all these differences informed our attitudes, we had all decided to live on Cliveden street, to commit half our incomes and much, much more toward making our own little world a bit closer to what we thought it should be—and now we were living with the satisfactions and the frustrations of that decision.

*   *   *

People who are considerably more possessive than we are couldn't very well adopt our style of living together. Take our cars as an example. For most Americans an automobile is some kind of projected self-image. But what a beating our ego symbols take, our half-assed fleet of economy vehicles being driven by so many people in so many styles. Pete drives hard and fast, and Chris is so loose that from time to time one suspects he has forgotten where he is and what he's doing; there's a suggestion of panic to Leigh's driving, and a flippancy to Ruth's; one moment I drive with exasperating indifference, and the next I'm taking foolhardy risks; Anne concentrates on her driving, Gary is considerate of his vehicle and other drivers alike, and Dan is always proper. Despite the cost to the lives of the cars and the peace of mind of their owners, it wasn't ever suggested that we stop regarding them as if they belonged to all of us. We didn't, in conversation, refer to Pete's car or Mike and Ruth's car, but rather to the Toyota or the Volvo. Still, although we shared all car-related expenses we didn't really assume equal responsibility for repairs, so that Gary and Anne, for instance, were the people who were aware when the VW needed some work, and saw to it, although somebody else in the house might drop the car off at the repair shop, or help Gary work on it. So protective attitudes remained, and Anne felt some disgust at times about the wear and tear on the VW, and so did Pete about the Toyota. The Mercedes and the Volvo had such tenuous grips on life that Leigh, Ruth, and I could all be a bit cavalier about the way they were treated.

You got to use a car if you needed one or wanted one, regardless of whether or not you owned it. If you were going to work, or a medical appointment, or a political meeting you could pretty much count on having a car. And we had enough cars so that you almost always could have one to go to a movie or to visit friends or away for a weekend, too. There were hardly ever times when some body wanted a car and there wasn't one available.

"The cars," Ruth said during one of our daily talks about who needed which vehicle to go where, "are a huge pain in the ass. If there were another way–self-propulsion or something– I'd prefer it." Despite the complications of sharing the cars, none of us was ready to suffer the ecologically sound inconvenience of doing without them.

Our other possessions fell into three categories of use: personal and private, personal but borrowable, and communal. Whatever you kept in your room was personal, and either private or borrowable depending on what you want ed. So that: the women all wore each other's blouses and sweaters, but the men didn't borrow one another's clothing at all, except for belts. So that: you could ask to use Steve's tent or Gary's camera, which were in their rooms, or a book kept by a bedside, or even a room itself if it was unoccupied. But: the books in the living room, and the records, and the stereo system, though they were all privately owned, were used communally. So that: Anne's rocker in the living room was communal, Anne's rocker in her bedroom was private. We furnished the house pragmatically: everything that was living room furniture went into the living room, including a couch from Gary and Anne, an easy chair from us, and so on. Posters and paintings dis played around the house came from each of us, as did vases and plants and random *tchotkes*. We built our dining-room table and everybody with dining-room-style chairs stuck them in the dining room. Into the kitchen and pantry went the plates and bowls and cups, except that Gary and Anne put their dishes away for safekeeping. Everybody else seemed to think that was okay, although if there hadn't been more than enough dinnerware among the rest of us perhaps we would have objected.

Material matters which had to be talked about were, sooner or later. But matters of principle rather than practice were never resolved at house meetings. Implicit in bringing any issue to the group was a willingness to accept a group decision if one was reached. If you wanted to avoid a group decision you simply didn't bring it up; if somebody else wanted to talk about it, though, you were stuck. There was never a time, so far as I can recall, when anybody said they wouldn't talk about a question of money or possessions. Perhaps the group would have accepted that answer, but I suspect not.

*   *   *

We took turns acting as the house bookkeeper; when it was your month to serve you had to pay all the bills, see to it that paychecks were deposited, keep the checkbook balanced, and make sure there was always cash on hand. This task came quite naturally to some of us, but not to Ruth, who was the kind of person who could write a half-dozen checks without thinking about it. She was compelled to look upon sitting down with the house check book as a form of sacred duty. She would work, in prayerful silence, at the dining-room table, looking harried but determined. Working on the accounts she reminded herself of her great-grandpa who had insisted on complete silence when he ate a fish in order to concentrate on not swallowing a bone.

We were, in a lot of ways, pretty loose about how we handled money. We kept our petty cash–which usually amounted to one hundred dollars a week or more–sitting in plain view in a blue ceramic cup on a kitchen shelf. We were so lax about it that when we were robbed of sixty-five dollars we didn't know it had happened until the thief owned up several days later. The confession came as a surprise: one night Matt seemed upset and when I asked him whether something was wrong he began to cry and finally told me that he had done something for which I would be unable to forgive him. The story, as it unfolded, was that he and a pal had decided to run away from home, and Matt had stolen the money and buried it in the backyard to finance the caper. We dug up the mouldy greenbacks and also found a plastic bag full of dog food for Gussie, who the kids planned on taking along for protection. Ruth and I had a long talk with Matt, and then we took it up at a house meeting, with Matt there. The outcome was that he was reprimanded and punished. He was told that by taking the money he had violated the trust which made living together possible, and we learned, the hard way, that he wasn't entirely happy on Cliveden street. A few weeks later he told us he wanted an allowance. I thought it over and decided that a dollar a week was probably about right for an eight-year-old who was stealing the folded stuff, not nickels and dimes. We asked him how much he wanted.

"Sixty-three cents," he responded without hesitation. And sixty-three cents he got.

Several months later, when Gary and Anne had told us of their decision to leave and the emotional and physical spaces that would be created by their departure were beginning to seem real, we began to talk about whether or not to add new people to the house. One issue in that discussion was that Pete thought that in order to meet our house budget we would have to replace nearly all of the income we would be losing. Leigh and I both disagreed with his argument. Dan would be beginning his internship and so earning about ten thousand dollars, or close to half the amount we would be losing; Leigh and I thought we could get by on what we'd have.

"We've gotten into this attitude," Leigh said, disagreeing with Pete, "that we need a huge financial cushion. What was once luxury is becoming our standard of living."

I was in accord with Leigh. "The way we live now." I maintained, "is that pretty much everything I want I can go out and get. I could live more frugally without any great feeling of deprivation."

That we could have this kind of candid disagreement indicated to me that income sharing was working the way we hoped it would. We were managing our money by mutual consent, and with a minimum of individual possessiveness. It wasn't eliminating differences entirely, but it was promoting greater equality.

"Income sharing," Ruth had decided, "is the most liberating thing in the world. For a very long while I considered money an embarrassment–and it gets in the way of so much. Now, when I have it I spend it; when I don't, I don't usually miss it. If the house has enough money to run on I don't care who it comes from. It comes in, it goes out. It's a very cyclical system."

Maybe income sharing was working because we had more than enough to live on without worry or inconvenience; or because we got along well, wanted a lot of the same things, and found that we could help each other get them. Maybe. But I don't really know.

Men

Why would men want to live communally, five of us under
one roof, none the man of the house? I've found that
competing to be the provider for my family, assuming a pose
of strength or wisdom regardless of my real state of mind and
heart, maintaining a shrewd air–in short, living up to the usual
expectations for a man in our culture leaves me tense,
alternately depressed and elated, and out of touch with my
own nature. It was only when I began to question and slowly
to relinquish some of my bogus claims to manhood, like so
many plastic credit cards enticing me with the easy delusion
that paying later is the same as not paying at all, that I began
to find some deeper-lying, more satisfying aspects of my
manliness. I think that I was a compliant victim of the
falsehood that manliness is achieved in a man's relationships
with women, that women validate a man's nature. This, for
instance, is one aspect of the message to men in a magazine
like Playboy. Women become a kind of prey (bunnies) for
man the hunter, not so much objects as lesser animals. When
the hunter lures a lot of prey into his traps, he is validated–
strong, masculine, virile.

In a society where it is more acceptable to be drunk than
sober if I am expressing my affection by hugging another man,
it is necessary to create ways of claiming my masculinity *with,*
not *from*, other men, in fellowship and not competition. It is as
if all the fine, soft things about men–our gentleness, our
kindness, our understanding, our playfulness–must be hidden.
Meanwhile, we are pressured to maintain the pretense that our
hard, strong characteristics–our aggressiveness, our

outspokenness, our durability and physical strength, our participation in the affairs of the world–are all that we are. The appeal to me in living with four other men was that I could learn to enjoy the fullness of myself with them, and together we could learn more of our mutual nature. Pete made love with a lot of different women, and that was part of my nature, too, though subordinated to my greater desire to commit myself to one woman, just as he, too, wanted a mate. Chris made love with other men, and that wasn't foreign to my feelings, nor was heterosexuality to his. The first time I was aware of having a sexual response to another man I was hugging Dan during an emotional house meeting in the fall. I had just told him that I trusted his kindness, but that I was also intimidated by the beauty and grace of his body; he leaned over and put his arms around me and when we hugged, sprawled awkwardly on the floor, I felt the sexuality and the restraint in our embrace.

There is a quality in most American men which comes, I suspect, from not being able to acknowledge the child who still lives within us, buried, squelched, denied, but still in there, snickering and giggling, being outrageously daring, dismayingly chicken, and a thoroughgoing wise-ass. That boy, that child who grew up without going away, is a disconcerting presence to a man who equates seriousness with solemnity and with manhood, which is the mentality of television situation comedy and of national politics. The irreverent, uncontrollable child of ourselves past, if unaccepted, has to be sat on hard. He's probably the leading cause of constipation, headaches and unsatisfactory orgasms. The kind of men identified as "national leaders" and "celebrities" all too often appear to be puff-chested bullyboys whose faces tell me not only that they haven't grown up, but that they lie even to themselves and live in constant fear of being found out. That's how Richard Nixon strikes me, and Teddy Kennedy, Johnny Carson, and David Brinkley.

Until we become reconciled to ourselves we are driven to question, way down inside, the actuality of our strength, and, as if proving it to other people were the same as convincing ourselves, we are likely to behave as if every action taken is a test of whether we are masculine or whether we are weak—because, terrible as it is, those are the accepted opposites. How can we relax about our own resources when we're fed such an unending diet of crap about standing strong and solitary, so that the mere dropping of the pose awakens demons whose outpost is deep within our own consciousness, demons whose delight is in making us tremble that we might not be what we should be? We grow up believing that we will not be loved by other men, which eventually leaves us alienated from our friends and coworkers. And we also learn to expect that we won't be able to love other men, which keeps us alienated from our own true nature. Thus, our cultural models, if accepted, isolate most men from our real social and personal potentials.

These psychological pitfalls, dangerous enough to navigate by themselves, are to our inner lives what capitalism is to our work lives. For most American men, other men are a threat. The economic competition which is the motor force of capitalism keeps us on our guard against each other. Now, if you view other men as a threat, and your home as where you can indisputably be the person who knows more than anybody else about everything, the place where you can let your guard down and be secure in your own power, then you will hardly want to live with other men. It was always much easier for me to be with women—to believe that I would be understood, liked and respected. But I've been learning how much of what I thought I could only reveal to women I can also share with men friends, most especially with Gary. Together, after months of assaulting our cultural educations, we created some free space, some moments in which we were able to relax about ourselves because we extended that much acceptance to one another. Being with Gary at times like that was a relief.

He had, I knew, a large and perhaps distorted respect for me and the direction my life had taken, so that sometimes he rebelled against the ways in which I was pointing and to which he was attracted, but it was always an effort for him to disagree with me because of the emphatic way in which I argued. For my part, I admired his grasp of the concrete, was envious of his kindness. But as much as we enjoyed our friendship, we both had trouble believing in it. There were unmistakable impasses, sometimes we would hardly speak to each other for a week or two, and then we'd both be tentative and prickly when we were together again.

It was after a separation of this kind that we found ourselves sitting up late one night, talking in the kitchen long after everybody else was asleep. We were sitting across from each other at the kitchen table, Gary with his long legs stretched out over a corner of the table, and me with the balls of my feet pushing against the edge of the table so that my chair tilted back. We had been talking for hours and Gary was recalling his family and his childhood, feeling sentimental. He described his father as a warm robust man who was always goosing him on. Once, Gary recalled, his father bought him a bicycle, it was too big, but that didn't stop him from lifting his son onto the seat anyway and giving him a shove: off Gary sped, unable to stop that two-wheeler under him from spinning down the block toward . . . pre-med in three years flat! No clerk's life for him; no, he moved successfully, earnestly, from one station to another until there was an inexplicable halt. Over his family's objection he went to Berkeley for a year. He bought his first book to read, not study. He discovered Mozart. He was swept up in the turmoil of Berkeley in the early sixties, proud of his decision to go against his parents' wishes by getting off that two-wheeler and taking a look around.

Since then there had been many surprises, unexpected pleasures, unforeseen entanglements. Now he found himself in the kitchen of a commune talking intimately with a man who only six months before had been a stranger, and intimidating to boot.

"It's so hard to accept your friendship," he said to me softly, and paused, characteristically, as though gathering his reserve. He swung his legs down oil' the table, crossed them in front of him and went on. "Every time we've talked recently I've felt an urge to tell you how much I care about you," he said. "I wonder if that's why we've spent so little time together the last few weeks, maybe I've been avoiding you?"

"Maybe," I said, and smiled.

"I get so tied up in doubts and 'thoughts' that I can't bring myself to talk to you," he continued.

Gary inspired me to live up to his idea of me, which was sometimes a strain, but also a reason to love him. "You know," I said, pushing a salt shaker from one spot to another, "neither you nor Anne has ever said that you love me."

"Maybe that's because I don't trust myself," he answered, looking at me across the table. "I know that there's really a warm spot in me for you and sometimes I get a glance at its magnitude and it really scares me."

"God, we really feed off each other's insecurities, you know what I mean?" I said, rocking slightly.

"We do, don't we," he laughed. "It's been a long time since I've thought I loved another man," he said, contemplatively. "Part of what bothers me, I guess, is that it's hard to think that I could feel the same way about someone that I did about Stephen–my friend who died of cancer."

"I'm really just starting to get a sense of how hard these kinds of expressions of affection are for you," I said. "I never realized that you seem so warm and encompassing." I relished the maudlin sentimentality of our friendship, two big, confident men with all the hesitation of inexperienced lovers. "But I know I feel . . . softly about you," Gary said intently, leaning forward and resting his elbows on the table. "But sometimes–and unpredictably–you can be very unsoft. Or I imagine you will be."

I looked at the light red, downy hair growing over the back of his hands.

"I go through love/hate cycles in regard to you," I said, wanting to put my hand over his, but not allowing myself, wanting to touch his big hand with mine. "Attraction/repulsion cycles, where one moment I'm drawn to you and the next repelled. At times I can't imagine not continuing to live with you, but then at other times I think, what a stupid dream, I can't tolerate living with Gary, he's impossible, he brings me down, he's always making demands on me"–I was speaking rapidly, on the trail of a thought–"he won't leave me alone– that's it! You don't leave me alone, Gary, and I love you for that and hate you for it too. You press me. You're hard work, like everything important is for me. You know what I mean?"

He laughed warmly. "When you say, 'You know what I mean like that it's almost impossible to disagree with you. It's like I'm following your thought and thinking about my reaction and then you say 'You know what I mean' so intently and I find myself saying, 'Yeah, sure, Mike, I know what you mean.'"

"I know what you mean," I said, unintentionally, and we both laughed.

There was a long, indwelling silence.

"I get into reveries of dreaming about a possible future together," Gary said softly, his Semitic face worried. "I wonder about what it'll be like when you meet my folks and my brothers–whether you'll get along."

It was as if everything in the pitch black world outside the pool of yellow light in which we sat had receded. Ours was a romantic, even a sexual cloistering. We were timid but also amused, delighted by our mood, our talk. I was full of night dreams, confiding. "Yeah," I said, slowly, my voice low. "I have this fantasy of standing outside a beautiful log house–a whole cluster of log houses–under a clear sky on a very green bluff overlooking the Pacific. I'm hoeing a garden–I've got a long, white beard–and I look up from the work I'm doing and up the road, in the distance, I can see this figure approaching, raising dust on the road–and I watch for a minute and then I see it's your son, I recognize him and I shout. He's maybe twenty years old, coming home from being on the road for the first time, and I drop my hoe and run down the road and we hug, we're so glad to see each other–we've lived together his whole life."

"God, that just blows my mind," Gary exclaimed, and gripped my hand in his.

"I'm enjoying myself more than I can say, just sitting here, talking like this," I said, squeezing his hand.

"To finally allow myself my feelings about you," Gary said, smiling but solemn, "provides me with . . . almost a triumph. Does that make sense?"

*   *   *

I live with other men, then, simply because I don't know another way to be so happily among men, don't know how else to learn so enjoyably what it means to be a man. The massive, impersonal institutions where most men work stopped offering me anything I wanted, and that was why I had to quit newspapering. In their hierarchies, their sly, unspoken competitiveness, their lack of self-examination, their indifference to the usefulness of what they produce, their bureaucratic ignorance of the full person, they fail me. As for our blood families, some crunch of the imperatives of capitalism, of bigness and richness and technology seems to have denied us those fine, loving places where men could mix in courage and skill and intelligence. We move too often and too many kinds of distances: we are separated from our kin. In the past men have traditionally learned about their own nature in those extended families which grew into clans or tribes or settlements. I don't see that we have as yet created any substitutes, certainly not a commune where the adults are all of one generation and there is a single child. But building such a community is one of my goals.

What many men turn to, looking for this kind of companionship, are play and sport. But what has happened, sadly enough, is that beyond boyhood we are either paid for our play or participate vicariously, as spectators. I learned everything I ever needed to know about professional sport when Walter O'Malley took my fantasy life to Los Angeles in order to make money. Schoolyards end empty fields and city streets are the places of real sport and play in America, and their rites are the rites of initiation. They no longer offer me what I want, although they did, gloriously, when I was a boy, and they can still be good fun.

Well, the year began with live of us, live men, as part of a single, intentional household. Deep voices, hard muscles, man hair growing over our bodies, our faces. All of us were mature enough to be fathers, to be the heads of our own families. Man smells and man laughter, cocks and balls between our legs. Who would be the poppa?

Not Chris. He was the youngest, the least experienced. And because he made love with men he would not have any children, would be denied that link to the future. Nor Dan, who was still a student, whose conflicts with his origins were too deep, as yet, to afford him acceptance of differences. Nor Pete, who was mate-less. I was the father of the only child, but my quest, in the winter of 1971, was to lay claim to my right to be weak; my confidence in my own resourcefulness was eroded, I lacked resonance. No, not me. Perhaps then it was Gary. He was married and intended soon to be a father, he was steadfast, he was large enough and strong enough, and his bushy moustache and long hair gave him a patriarchal look.

Certainly Pete was an uncle in our ersatz family: a few years older, unattached–a bachelor uncle. He was responsible, commonsensical, and could be stern, although his sternness sometimes masked a playful impulse. "I guess I'm not the warm and cuddly sort," he said grumpily. But despite himself he was a favorite uncle, liked and respect ed. There were moments when I wanted to reach out and muss Pete's hair, but was stopped by embarrassment. All the hugging that sometimes swelled over the dam of our reserve–hugging in the kitchen out of sheer happiness at being together, hugging Matt in great big kiss and cuddle hugs–brought out Pete's mock sternness. "Jesus," he would mutter, "physicality is rampant in this household." Which got him a hug, too.

But it was hard for him to live with three couples. Watching Ruth and me, Gary and Anne and Dan and Leigh working our ways through our problems and somehow always back to our loves made Pete afraid that he was too lazy, or uninvolved, to commit himself to such a recurring struggle. He watched Ruth and me yell at each other, hurt each other, and then, slowly, regain the ground where we rid ourselves of our bitterness and it caused him greater longing than anything else in his life. At times like that he felt alone among nine people. He envied Gary and Dan and me for what we had. And his reaction to living with couples was a surprise to him, as it was to me. We had all assumed that the greater envy would be on the part of the settled, married men watching Pete free to follow his sexual whims. And, in fact, he went with a lot of women, passing rapidly from one liaison to another, sometimes more than one going on simultaneously. He kept his life outside the house very much to himself, there was something of the gambler in him, he played his cards close to his vest. But he had always been like that, even when he was a teenager he never talked to the other guys about the girls he knew, never trusted the way his buddies treated girls, teachers, the odd guy out. There was always the suspicion in Pete that he was next–perhaps he even deserved to be next–that if he let too much of himself show he would be mercilessly handled. Moving into the house was an act of courage for him in ways that it wasn't for me.

It was at a house meeting in January that Pete began to feel tremors of uncertainty sweeping along the taut line of his reserve. Gary was telling us, with a troubled, dreamy urgency, of a time when "a fissure opened up, and I slid through it," and as Gary tumbled through dreams and recollections, Pete recalled the long, cozy drive he and Gary had made after a ski trip, alone together in the car from Montreal back to Philadelphia, barreling through the cold, barren, snow-covered mountains of western New York. There was no place he was more comfortable than behind the wheel of his car–traveling on. How fondly he remembered the secure feeling of the two of them, the two men. They talked about a woman they had met–she was pretty, with dark black hair cut short, smiling eyes, and a French-Canadian accent . . . for her these bushy Anglos were as much a romantic curiosity as she was to them. Both of them were charmed by her and her interest in them. A week with the smell of the winter forest in their nostrils had cleansed their senses, sharpened their appetites. Yes, yes, yes, yes, yes. And in the intimacy of the long car ride home Gary had told Pete how he worried that Pete always seemed to be drawn to women who were living in another city, or with another man, or . . .

"There's always something," Gary had said, "that keeps you from getting involved."

Pete had objected. It was such a drag to have the afterglow of his week dimmed by this conversation. But even so he remembered having thought how much caring Gary expressed for him time and time again, how he made Pete feel capable of reciprocating in kind. Recalling that drive as he sat in the house meeting listening to Gary, he bided his time.

"Since I've grown up I've cried in front of my mother twice," Gary concluded. "The first time was at the funeral of my friend Stephen, and she made me stop. The other time she left."

"Where does that leave you now?" Pete asked.

As they began to talk, Pete questioning Gary, trying in his way to manifest his desire for Gary's happiness, I found myself beginning to get angry. It sounded to me as if Pete were probing, detached—risking very little of his own psychic currency. I had been moved by what Gary said, and now, distressed by the unexpected vehemence of my reaction, I escaped into my own reverie, worrying about the suddenness and force of my anger at Pete. What I recalled was a house meeting several weeks before. Ruth and I had been fighting— the venom, the frustration flooded back over me—and Leigh had been talking to both of us, trying to help. I felt cornered and ferocious because I detested my own public display and when Leigh said something which wasn't precisely sympathetic with my point of view I lashed out at her angrily. I must have done that a number of times, I was only dimly aware of it, when Leigh finally objected, her voice trembling with rage and hurt.

"I'm not going to say another word," she said. "I'm pulling out. I can't stand up under that level of attack, Mike."

Yes, there was a menace to my anger, it was an effective way of protecting my psychic territory, or of intimidating my neighbors. The tide of my anger against Pete broke mightily over the beachhead of that understanding, and ebbed. And in its wake I found that I wasn't angry at Pete at all, but frustrated by the caution which separated us. I knew that if I spoke with anger I would succeed at nothing but driving Pete even further away. And that, truly, wasn't what I wanted. I sensed that Pete, by engaging Gary, had left himself invitingly open. And his vulnerability put me to the test—how much easier to smash him for provoking me to confront myself than to accept his invitation—whether or not it was intended for me. And it wasn't intended for me, after all, but there it sat, his conversation with Gary at an end, and I snatched it up.

"Pete, sometimes I feel as though there's an enormous distance between us," I said, and I let loose an internal sigh of relief, because I could hear that I, too, was inviting. "I admire you. Especially for the way you've fought through to a lot of self-acceptance. But the feeling I had just now when you were talking to Gary was that when you do reach out it's often with dicta or conclusions you've reached, and not with the experiences you've gone through that taught you what you know. And so I began to get the feeling—and this wasn't the first time—that you hide behind your answers as well as believe them."

I could hear what I wanted in how I said my piece. And Pete responded at once. He had been sitting on the couch, weaving on a hand loom he had made out of sticks. He put down the loom.

"The most difficult thing . . ." he began, in a strained voice, and then stopped and thought. He was afraid of his own temper, felt unable to trust his own feelings. How hard it was to trust a man like me: he had never trusted men with authority, never.

"I've basically been a very autocratic person who is resistant to taking advice," he said, in a slow, in-looking way. "I tend to reject a lot of things from other people. It's been my experience that I know best for myself." And now there was another pause, while he gathered himself up for an admission he had not expected to make. Gains in consciousness were so painful. "What I've found most difficult to accept about myself since I've lived here is when I don't react, when I don't open myself up," he said. "I worry that I'm an accommodator, that if I open myself up too completely yield very quickly to group pressure."

"I'm surprised," I said more confidently, "because you've been the most outspoken person in the house about holding yourself out."

"That came from fear," Pete said, and I noticed then that his hands were trembling.

And in that moment, when each of us waged a private war to trust himself, some small element of trust for each other emerged, and we spoke now more rapidly, with a friendly respect.

"I always thought that came from a place inside you where you were really certain of yourself," I said with surprise. "I always felt defensive when you expressed your individuality so strongly, because one of the things I don't like about myself is that I blow with the wind."

"You?" Pete asked incredulously, with an almost-smile. "You seem so intractable. You say, 'Okay, if the group wants it I'll go along with it, but I'm good and pissed off.' I've admired you for that and hated you at the same time. I don't think I've expressed my reservations as strongly. Lots of times I don't stand up for my rights."

So much talk, Pete thought, he had so little faith in it. And it embarrassed him. Always, when he thought back to what he had said and done in the past he asked himself: was I really like that? It was hard to get past self-pride, to stop looking for answers, to just let life unfold. He distrusted his answers as he gave them, they mutated on the spot.

"We all go on being ourselves," he said. "Things are going to work out the way they're going to work out."

"When you say things like that," Anne cried, "I feel as though I could walk out of your life tomorrow and you wouldn't care at all."

In the weeks that followed, Pete seemed more receptive to the rest of us than ever before and yet he remained the same. He still held himself back severely–I still sensed a realm of unexplored pain and regret somewhere within him. Knowledge of its presence made him seem sad, just out of reach. Yet one day he walked into the kitchen, began buttering a piece of toast, and said; with no preface: "I don't think I could ever live by myself again."

It made me laugh.

"You're too fucking much," I said.

*　　*　　*

Then there was Matt, the boy, the man-to-be. How did he fare among five grown-up men? Certainly he had more diverse models in his own home for what a man was like than most boys do. He was part of a household which included diffident as well as aggressive men, pensive as well as active men, men of science and men of arts, men who danced, sang, sewed, sawed, fixed cars, baked, gardened; men who held jobs and men who didn't, men with mates and men without mates.

Perhaps even more important was my place in the household, because, even though I was influential and sometimes dominant, I was not, as I've said, the man of the house, not some model of unchallenged strength and infallibility. Matt was aware that my logic and my beliefs were not unassailable, that what I thought sometimes prevailed and sometimes didn't. He saw that other men were some times angry or impatient with me, but that at other times they were respectful and affectionate toward me. He had an opportunity to see me pretty fully and clearly in relation to other men, and I couldn't help but be glad for that.

There were good times and bad for him among the men. He remembers the day that he and Gary took off on the motorcycle, riding out into the country where they walked to the edge of a slimy green swamp. "Let's call it Creamed Spinach Swamp," Matt suggested, and they did, playing Indians around its shoreline until they were hungry and went to the airport and devoured hamburgers and ice cream while they watched the jet planes take off for faraway places. Then there were the more difficult times. Like the time he walked into the kitchen while Gary and I were having it out over something or another, shouting loudly and belligerently at each other from our full heights. Matt was glad to scoot out of the way, grateful that we were booming at each other and not at him.

*   *   *

Somehow Chris was treated like a child, more a sibling to Matt than to the rest of us. Sensing Chris' ambivalence about his own authority, Matt would let loose on him more as an equal, and the two of them would sometimes get into shouting recriminations, often in the kitchen. But they also had fun together, and Chris taught Matt how to make pastries, one of Matt's proudest accomplishments.

During one of the few private, intimate conversations I had with Chris I told him that I was troubled by the way I crowded him out of the picture. "When I'm annoyed at you I'll usually treat you the way I'd treat a kid," I said, apprehensively.

"I let you do it, too," Chris said, relieved to have it out in the open. "I've been conscious of it, but I haven't been able to bring it up. I think I really see myself as a kid sometimes. There are some things I do which really freak me out. Like asking for a men's room I suddenly feel like a sixteen-year old asking for his parents' car. Since I don't project a lot of male things–like anger or loudness–people who are up tight can deal with me like I'm a kid."

Like Chris, Dan, too, was something of an outsider. He wasn't included in what Ruth half-mockingly and half seriously described as the "council of elders" when she saw Pete, Gary, and me, all three of us with bushy beards and solemn Jewish faces, talking our way intently down a city street, like secular rabbis in a New World *shtetl*.

Pete and Dan grew to care and admire for each other, but Gary and Dan had difficulty even understanding each other's languages. Gary was glad for the occasional ease of their comradeship, but it was a pain in the ass for him to feel stuffy and uptight, and Dan's laconic responses to him often made him feel just that way.

In a group of people for whom, as Ruth said, "the medium of exchange is a heavy rap," Dan virtually never talked about behavior directly or personally, and certainly never drew upon it as a source of humor. Though he could be remarkably good-natured and agreeable, I don't ever remember having heard Dan laugh.

One Sunday when he wasn't working his usual long, physically and emotionally draining day in the hospital, he got up with the sun, put on dungarees, and barefooted and bare-chested, built a slow-burning fire in the living room. He smoked some grass, stacked an enormous pile of records (Roy Acuff and the Smokey Mountain Boys are his favorites) on the stereo, and settled in for the day. As time went by he danced for hours, then curled up like a pretzel in his own improvised yoga positions, and finally, he stood swaying back and forth looking far away out of the window or into the embers of the fire. He thought about how hard he had tried to make a life in the city, how successful he'd been in some ways, drawing closer to people, becoming a doctor. And he thought of his family, how his father worked hard all his life, never letting things get him down. Man, he told himself disgustedly, sometimes you think you got it rough. Shieeet! He was the second son, but his father, a hard-driving man, put Dan in charge when there was work to be done. In leaving to go to college, in succeeding in his own ambitions, had he disappointed his father's ambitions for him?

He knew that he had only one life to live and what he wanted was to go back to Lebanon, or someplace like it, and put his roots down in some rich, black soil. He knew that he was preparing himself to live where his kids could run around and feel the real freedom, so that they could know what he felt like when he was standing on a hill and looking out over the fields, just watching it all and knowing what it was like to work there with the people and to help things grow. But it scared him, too, because he had changed, and the world back home hadn't—or at least not in the same ways.

Raised in a world where smoking, drinking, dancing and movies were sinful, he had come to the big city and lived with people with too much education, people who didn't work with their hands, people who he had been taught to mistrust. He had become a doctor with an Ivy League education living in a commune with a woman who wasn't his wife. His parents, whom he loved and honored, did not want any of the other Yoder children to go to college. "Look what it's done to Daniel," his mother observed.

He interrupted his reverie to munch on a tuna sandwich that he had brought into the living room that morning wrapped in a plastic bag so he wouldn't have to leave the fire and the music for lunch. But as he chewed he thought, and the tension persisted between his past and his present. He understood that in its resolution was the path to his unknown future.

Couples

Sometimes I saw the three couples in our house on a continuum: Dan and Leigh didn't know if they wanted a future together; Gary and Anne were committed, but worried that they might not win the intimacy they sought; Ruth and I grew dissatisfied when we saw our individuality submerged in the totality of our marriage. All of us had said that we would welcome some helpful interference from the other people in the house. Yet, of course, the prospect was intimidating: the privacy of a marriage, or of a man and woman together, was sacrosanct, and we were all worried that our own garbage smelled worse than anybody else's.

Perhaps because they were the least certain of what they had to offer each other, Dan and Leigh had the most public relationship. At times both of them would seem to despair. Leigh would say she saw no way they could stay together and grow as individuals, and Dan would fall into a glowering, hurt silence. For days and sometimes weeks at a time they would move separately through their own lives, friendly but apart. Until one day I would happen upon them in the living room wrestling and nuzzling and laughing; but even then, even when they teased and played and were happy together, I couldn't see how the satisfactions they offered one another were enough to keep them together despite their differences.

As the winter began, Leigh was working hard and the two of them were seldom spending time together. They reconnected after Christmas and, pleased with themselves, decided to take a vacation in the Caribbean. But just a few nights before they were due to leave their mood changed

again, their plans lurched back and forth, and in the midst of
their uncertainty a friend of theirs was invited along on their
trip. They had never taken a spell of time alone, away from
everybody they knew. Though neither of them acknowledged
it, I thought that the presence of the friend defused the
prospect of having only each other for company. They
wondered if they would be bored with each other during the
weeks in the hot sun. And I suspected that it frightened them
both–frightened them too badly to talk to each other about it–
that neither of them knew, really, if they wanted each other or
just the security of having somebody.

They were ready to fight when they came to the house
meeting several days before their departure. The prospect tired
me: though I wanted to help, I always sensed a hollowness to
their battles, something was lacking, some certainty that what
they had was worth fighting for, perhaps. I wasn't sure. But
they were a bit too self-conscious, they lacked passion. It was
as if they had tacitly agreed always to hold something back,
never to hurt each other too dreadfully nor to love each other
too passionately. They had an unspoken compact for restraint
which remained undemolished because it had never been
assaulted by dread or rage or fever. And so nothing was ever
settled by their fights, the possibility of greater risks never
resulted.

"It's a drag not anticipating the vacation," Dan said in the
high, pinched way he sounded when he was argumentative.
"Half the fun I've always had doing things is just planning
them. I've felt pushed and crowded and just not really excited
by the whole thing."

"I haven't got any clear idea what you're resistant to,"
Ruth said. Despite the discomfort she sometimes felt with Dan
she also found that they could talk together before and after a
crisis. But when calm was lost, so was their capacity to hear
each other.

"It's like a whole attitude I have toward world travel," he
replied. "I'm not used to it. That sort of thing was always
something that other kinds of people did."

"What kinds?" Ruth interrogated him.

"Well, people with a lot of money and nothing better to do with their lives," he laughed sheepishly, and pulled the blanket he was holding a bit tighter around his shoulders. "Even like when I mentioned to my mother on the phone that I was going to the Caribbean I got a sense of how the wheels were turning in her head."

"I don't think it's a particularly rational kind of reaction that you're having," Ruth said easily.

"I guess if I really felt it was rational and logical I wouldn't be going," Dan answered. But when Leigh began to talk he looked sullen.

"I don't feel it's assumed that we are going, right now," Leigh said, choking on her words. "I just feel so shitty about it . . . I just don't know how I feel."

I sensed her desire to lash out at Dan, to blanket him with her anger, and then she pulled herself up short.

"I just don't want to feel that I railroaded you into it," she said. "I guess one of the things that did happen is that I fucked up, I knew you were reluctant and I pushed what I wanted to do, go to the Islands and lie in the sun. I guess I assumed you were getting into it when you got the brochures and everything . . ." I wished she would stop being so goddamn reasonable and let herself go, because I was sure that in a part of herself she almost always kept in check what she wanted to do was slug the pigheaded bastard.

"On the other hand," she continued, growing more confident, "I was also going on the basis of something, which was that we were planning on going somewhere together until you popped up one night and said you were going to a farm for the two weeks and I could come along if I wanted to. I keep getting hit with all these new decisions all the time and I never know when I'm standing on solid ground with you. I can never tell what's just a fantasy and what's not, so I'm reacting to one thing one week and another the next week."

She paused to light a cigarette–she had never smoked until that fall. I knew that whether she reacted to Dan's ever-shifting plans and moods, or whether she bulldozed her way through, she ended up suspecting there was something wrong with her. Again and again and again she found herself caught between being the passive object of Dan's will, or a shrill, accusing bitch. And she detested the thought of being either.

"I always feel at sea with you," she said introspectively. "Maybe I'm demanding too much . . . I don't know."

Anne could hardly wait to speak her mind: she knew only too well what it meant to be in love with a stubborn, mulish man.

"These last few weeks," she said to Dan, "Leigh's been telling me that the two of you feel much more of a commitment to an ongoing relationship. And then I hear unilateral decisions coming down like, 'Look, I'm going to a farm, take it or leave it.' Dan, I don't understand if you care about Leigh how you make all the decisions on your own without including her?"

"I really had the feeling that you were out to get me at the house meeting tonight," Dan said to Leigh, sounding patient but bitter. "My perception of the last couple of weeks is that I've really tried to spend time with you but the problem is that you're never around here. That's why decisions are made unilaterally," he added, turning toward Anne. "I think it's unfair to lay that on me."

If Leigh made it hard for Dan to fall back behind the anger which was his most comfortable retreat, if she tied him in more complex knots by blaming herself for what he secretly suspected might be his fault, then his aim was just as shrewd: nowhere was she more vulnerable than in the suspicion that she didn't put out enough, that the problem was in the meagerness of what she had to offer. Yet neither of them was calculating, both were genuinely angry, genuinely repentant.

"Well, I guess you're right about some of that," Leigh answered. "I find myself tearing into your fantasies, putting them down. I was reluctant to bring this up tonight because I have so much anger toward you I was afraid that I'd just be out to get you . . ."

Go get him then, I wanted to shout, but didn't.

"On the other hand," she continued, her voice losing its edge of bitterness, "I thought it would be better to bring it up where people can help us."

"I don't know why," Anne said angrily, "Leigh can't tell you to fuck off when you come down with one of your fantasies, like going to the farm for your vacation. You know they're going to get a rise out of Leigh. They keep her at arm's distance."

A smile almost flickered across Dan's angry, beset expression. "I know the distance is there," he said abruptly.

The tempo of the exchanges was quickening, the submerged anger was closer to the surface.

"It's like you see commitment to a woman being like your parents' lifelong way, come hell or high water, no questions asked," Anne said excitedly. "And Leigh can't imagine making a commitment to a man, she thinks they're all like her father–zero dependability."

"I still feel so bummed out by this whole thing that I'd almost rather stay in Philadelphia and work," Leigh said dully. "I don't see how we're going to have any fun if you don't want to go."

Dan was neatly fixed on the point of Anne's anger while Leigh twisted the blade in the core of his guilt.

"I don't know where to go from here," he said sharply. "How can you expect me not to have the feelings I do? Once I'm on the plane stop hassling it and have a good time."

"If you know you're not going to be miserable," Anne shouted at him, "why don't you cut it out?"

That was all he was willing to take. "Well, I'm sorry, but that's what I feel," he shouted in a high, dry, angry voice.

"Okay," Gary shouted–he had to yell in order to be heard, suddenly everybody was talking at once–"you've brought that out. Now why are you keeping it up?"

Dan was without an ally, and he got even louder since he would have to produce all the force of his argument on his own. "I'm pissed because she's making me go down there and I didn't really want to go."

"Whaaat!?" Anne shrieked. "She is *not* making you!"

Leigh remained silent.

"She *is* making me," Dan insisted, with more truth than anybody acknowledged. "So what am I going to do?" he asked himself out loud, the peak of his anger passed. "I really want to be with her these two weeks, it's really important to both of us."

Such an impersonal shyness that he should say, "I want to be with her," and not, "I want to be with you."

"I don't know," Leigh said wearily.

"We'll take the plane to the Islands and we'll have a really good time," Dan said, being conciliatory.

"Leigh," said Ruth, "you have the option of making the best you can of your doubts and ending up with the vacation you wanted, pretty much. You ought to see how you're feeling in the next day or two."

Finally, Leigh began to cry. "We never get off the fucking merry-go-round. I feel like a broken record. It seems like we're not going anywhere."

"I guess I feel like there's a certain reality to the level of our commitment," Dan said.

They continued to sit apart from each other, they did not touch. Their argument had perhaps cleared the air, but it had quickened no understanding between them. They were stuck: with each other.

*　　*　　*

Gary and Anne were both so serious of purpose that their getting married implied a ceaseless effort to–in one of Gary's habitual phrases–work things out. Anne had decided to move into the house not only because the politics of a communal lifestyle was appealing, but because, as she had said, she wanted help in growing with Gary. Perhaps more precisely than anybody else in the group she under stood what she wanted. And I never failed to be impressed by how directly and bravely she and Gary went after what they wanted, and how the force of their determination shaped the emotional life of the house. But Anne's ties to the rest of us were ties of friendship more than of community. Her commitment to maintaining a community that would be more than temporary was weak, almost nonexistent. Yet, ironically, it seemed as though she were made for Communal living–nobody had better, more solidly committed friendships in the house than Anne did. In part that was because she was direct, even impetuous. A half-dozen times during the year Anne came up to me in haste and blurted out, "Are you angry at me about something?" or, "I want to tell you what I'm annoyed at you about." And her directness made it easy to live with her, I seldom suffered the uncertainty of having to puzzle out how she was feeling about herself, about me, about the house. More certainly than anybody else, she made herself felt in our individual lives. She spent time with each of the rest of us separately and privately, closeting herself away in her bedroom for long, frank talks.

As she began to accept the genuineness of the love and respect being offered to her by the people in the house it became easier for her to shift–slowly, very slowly–a balance which had always existed between her and Gary. If Gary was no longer bottled up, if he had opened new realms in himself, if he less often felt cornered or self-righteously angry, then it was just as true that she finally began to believe the obvious, began to believe that, truly, all the fuck-ups were not hers. They were beginning to recognize the real configurations of what they gave each other, they were responding to their emerging selves.

Living in the group they were more autonomous from each other, less exclusively reliant on each other for company, for entertainment, for understanding. And our communal arrangements had relieved Anne from the primary responsibility to cook and clean for both of them. Past that first wrenching battle and the decision to go into therapy together, the house was acting like a decompression chamber for their marriage. But in the middle of the winter they had to make a decision which stirred up many of Anne's accumulated resentments. Gary had a job offer in San Francisco, a chance to do a residency in community medicine that would give him the supervised training he wanted while also allowing him to do overtly political work in a companionable atmosphere. The job was more than just appealing, it was irresistible. But if he took it, that would mean that once again his work was disrupting their lives.

It had been ghastly for Anne when Gary did his internship in New York the year they were married. She had felt pulled up by the roots–her family, her friends, her job were all left behind. In New York Gary had always been at the hospital, and she had felt deserted. Even the following year when they lived in San Francisco she still had felt dislocated, every few months they would have bitter, destructive lights. At least, she had thought to comfort herself, we have time to argue. But just when she was beginning to settle into their life there, the government demanded its two years of service of Gary and shipped him (and Anne along with him, an appendage at most in this transaction) to Philadelphia. Again.

When Gary said he wanted to return to San Francisco in July, 1972, for the residency, all those accumulated grievances rushed to the surface–she refused to go. She was happy in Philadelphia, liked her job, was ready to have a baby, wanted to go on living in the house. They were both troubled by their impasse. Though we talked about it several times in house meetings, and they talked individually with the people in the house, it was apparent that they were going to make their decision on their own. Finally an alternative began to take form, a way past the deadlock. They would travel for a year, and then settle in San Francisco. Anne would get pregnant and they would have the baby on the Coast a few months before Gary's job began–that way he would be at home during the first part of their child's infancy. Each of them would be giving up something of what they wanted, and they wouldn't be forcing each other toward a showdown which they really didn't want.

For them it was a good decision. Anne thought that living in the house had provided her with invaluable support during this time. And she had gotten a sign from Gary that she was as important as his work, that he would sacrifice for her, even if only temporarily. Gary knew, too, that living in the house had made it impossible for him to simply insist that Anne was unreasonable in what she wanted. Sometimes he could hear her arguments more clearly when they were endorsed and expressed by one of the rest of us. And he was relieved to find that although we all wanted them to stay, no pressure was applied. His life was still his own. He thought that someday he might want to say to himself that where he lived and worked were decisions involving all these other people. But not yet.

Because they both felt so good about the way in which they had made their plans I thought I shouldn't be let down. I told myself that I should share their happiness, that the growth in their marriage seemed to confirm the usefulness of our commune, that for me, as for them, marriage ties were stronger than communal ties. And yet, I was more intimidated than persuaded by their reasons for leaving. I wanted to tell them that I didn't want them to break up the group, wanted to plead in behalf of the fulfillment of a future together. But by and large I kept my mouth shut and brooded. There was, unquestionably, a group pressure most often articulated by Pete–to be cool, to accept that it was inevitable that a man would place his work above other considerations, that a happy couple would sacrifice most anything else to keep what they had together. It's true that in their place I would probably have made the same kind of decision that they did, but I still wished I had spoken up more clearly about what was on my mind. I wished I had said that in order to build a community–and I want very badly to build a lifelong home–much that we have learned to consider most important has to be looked at from a new perspective. Our culture shapes our values, teaches us what happiness is. The effort to recreate ourselves in our own images is painfully vast, and it takes an unceasing commitment. Even if I had said all that I'm sure I wouldn't have been persuasive, but I would have been truer to what I was thinking, truer to what I believed. As it was, I felt the house was failing to some extent. If people shifted and moved and went on their solitary ways every year there was no future for a commune like ours. I had no intention of starting with a new group year after year, the cost was too high, the weariness too great. I was terribly let down to find that Gary and Anne didn't share my dream. Finally, one day, I just accepted the inevitable: after June we would be seven. I felt an enormous loss: I loved them dearly. And my resolve stiffened to find new people who had a kid about Matt's age.

* * *

Ruth was upstairs putting Matt to sleep during a house meeting in mid-January when he began to cry.

"What's the matter, Matt? What is it?" she asked, rocking him in her arms.

"Are Gary and Anne leaving the house?" he asked, between sobs.

Oh god, Ruth thought, eight years old, why does he have to go through this? "Probably they will be next summer," she said, stroking his hair.

"It's just like last year with Gil and Wendy," he said, during a pause while he tried to catch his breath. "Communal living . . . just isn't worth it . . . if . . . everybody keeps . . . going away."

"Yes," Ruth said, "yes, baby, I feel that way, too." She wanted to protect him from sadness, and here she had put him in the middle of an ever-changing grownup world. Shouldn't a kid feel that there are people he can depend on absolutely? She wondered, does he feel he can depend on me? When he was very young she had comforted herself by thinking that she was such a mess he would never have any false notions about her dependability or strength. But it was reassuring to her that he was pouring out his sadness to her.

"They're not leaving our lives entirely," she said. "They're going to drive around in their new camper and come back and visit us some, and then I'm sure we'll visit them in California, too."

Soon he calmed down and Ruth sat with him in the dark until he was drowsy. She kissed him on his warm, smooth forehead. "Good night, dear," she said softly. "Sleep tight."

She came back to the house meeting and waited for the first opportunity and then she said, "Matt was crying and kind of upset just now because he's picked up that Gary and Anne are going to be leaving and we haven't told him anything about it."

"Oh god," Gary said, "that's right, I haven't said any thing to him at all. God, I feel terrible."

Anne remembered a conversation they had had when she was driving Matt over to Jono's house. They had passed a microbus and she had said, "We may get one of those and travel, what color do you think would be good?" And Matt had asked, "Can I go with you?" Anne had replied, "Let's talk to your folks about that, we can probably go camping together for a while, maybe up in Canada." Then Matt had started to caution her about not buying a VW bus. "They tip over in the wind," he had said, "they're dangerous, you can get killed," and he had started to build one disastrous fantasy on top of the next until, finally, she had yelled, "Matt!"–loud enough, laughing enough, to stop him in his tracks, to bring him back. "If we go camping," he had asked, "how would I get home? You wouldn't just drop me off somewhere in the woods, would you?" "No," she had laughed, reassuring him. Now, suddenly, at the house meeting, she understood what he had been getting at: are you going to leave me?

"We *will* make some plans for him to travel with us and visit us in California," she said.

Ruth felt reassured by the apparent depth of Gary and Anne's concern. She was thinking about Gary, about how she would miss him, about how long it had taken for him to become a man with whom she was comfortable, although there still remained all sorts of empty spaces when they were together.

While Gary was talking about how we really didn't take Matt into account as a separate person in the house, Ruth thought that for most of her life she had accepted at face value everything, just everything, that people told them about themselves. Then, once she had begun to see that she could read other people, could speculate about what was really moving them, it had become a real kick, had slowly become what she wanted to do more than anything else. She realized now that Gary was undergoing a similar change. He had gone along in life thinking that he had no problems, that everything was under control. Like Mike, she thought, a lot like Mike. But when he found out that he could get into himself, explore himself in ways which he had never dreamed were possible, ways that he had always suspected were just a bit . . . well, unstable, there was no holding him back. He worked so hard at it, she thought. Earnest, overbearing Gary. Sometimes he wanted to help so much that he boxed her in. He pursued her about being indirect, about sending nonverbal messages that seemed to contradict what she was saying. Though she knew he was right, she also resisted his insistence.

"What's on your mind, Ruth?" Gary asked. "You look worried." Ruth left so much to his imagination, it made her very perplexing, very alluring. He wondered if she was blaming herself for Matt's upset. He thought that she was a good mother, Matt a great kid, the kind of kid he wanted himself. A real devil, he smiled to himself, he runs rough shod over authority.

"I'm okay," she said. "I'm just feeling pretty bad about Matt, you know?" She would miss Gary, miss him very much. She wanted him to stay, but didn't know how to say that without intruding. He was a comfort to her, trudging into our room, Doctor Gary, rubbing his head with his knuckles, talking to Mike or listening to us howl at each other . . .

*   *   *

These were rough times for Ruth and me, we were scraped raw. We had decided–mostly at my urging–that we were secure enough about each other to go to bed with other people without loosening our own ties. Six, seven, eight years together–we had begun to think and act alike. There was a lot of good humor between us, we absorbed a lot of anger by making each other laugh. We were closer to one another, more free in bed and out, more loving than either of us had ever been with anybody else. Secure that we were good together, we also knew that we didn't satisfy all of each other's needs; we both wanted more in dependence. We decided it would be okay to fuck other people before we left for Alaska the previous summer. It had seemed dreamlike, far away–though the prospect was exciting it had no immediacy, the consequences were hard to imagine.

When we got back to Cliveden street I was eager to bed somebody right away, before Ruth did. I became interested in a neighbor, Ruth was aware of me gravitating toward her. It worried her more than she wanted to admit. Late one night, unable to sleep, she went downstairs looking for company. Chris was asleep next to Dan on the carpet in front of the low-burning fire, where he had dozed off enjoying Dan's physical presence. Chris was feeling sensually content by the warm fire, when Ruth woke him by shaking his shoulder and whispering his name until he stirred.

"What's the matter?" he asked in a sleepy voice.

"I hope I'm not bothering you," Ruth said.

"No," he answered, stretching and yawning. He was startled to see Ruth, even more amazed that she wanted something from him.

"I'm having trouble sleeping," Ruth said. She was wearing a red flannel floor-length nightgown. "I'm feeling threatened by how much time Mike is spending with Lisa." She could see that Chris looked startled. What have I done? she asked herself.

He stroked her head, hugged her. Because she was a therapist he had assumed she had sexual jealousy all worked out and resolved. He worried about what he should say. After awhile he told Ruth about some past lovers who were especially important to him, memory moving in lazy three-in-the-morning loops. Listening, Ruth could hear Chris' depression at the briefness of his most important affairs. "That's just the way things are in the gay world," he said. "I don't like it very much."

"I don't know how you can be satisfied with one-night stands, Chris, you have so much more than that to give," Ruth said. She began to understand that the sympathy he always gave in such abundance was in proportion to what he wanted. She thought that that was Why he manifested such unconditional acceptance, why he was always ready to commiserate.

And, as Chris understood that all Ruth wanted from him was comfort, he relaxed. He had comfort aplenty to give to her: he felt his affection for her swelling up inside of him. Sometimes he felt in emotional synchronization with Ruth, especially when they were both sad. He hugged her, finding the warmth of her body against his reassuring. They sat like that, lost in their separate reveries, until Ruth went back upstairs to bed. Perhaps because we were accomplishing something Chris was afraid to want himself, he got a lot of satisfaction from watching Ruth and me together. He enjoyed our naturalness, our lack of embarrassment with each other, the ease with which we expressed our love. He admired the way we pushed each other, and how our anger seemed to cool as rapidly as it flared.

It was at about this time of the year that Ruth, who had been an instigator in the house, whose burst of committed energy had fueled the excited pace at which we got to know one another, began to withdraw. She spent more time alone than ever before. And she had a way of seeming so vulnerable and tired and unhappy that other people hung back from her, hesitated to intrude. Pete was frustrated by his inability to tell her how annoyed he was that she was shirking her responsibilities to the house, how hurt and disappointed he was, as well, to feel so cut off by her. He had expected to be close to Ruth, and now he found her the least approachable person in the house. Anne and Gary both told me that they felt baffled, powerless and tongue tied around Ruth.

Both Ruth and I had anticipated that she might become involved with some man in her training program, where the interaction was hot and heavy. In the weeks before Christ mas she began to be attracted to Martin, another trainee. He visited our house for dinner a few times, and I liked him. Martin was outgoing, not at all diffident. He and Ruth laughed a lot together. And he was several years younger than Ruth, in some ways less sure of himself. She felt a special satisfaction in being in control of their relationship. Just before Christmas Ruth asked me how I would feel if she went to bed with Martin. She was nervous, and felt like a child asking permission.

I said okay. I was apprehensive, but also excited, and if Ruth had an affair I thought it would make me feel easier about having one too. I was about to leave with some of the other people in the house on a week-long vacation in the mountains, and Ruth, who had to work until mid-week, was planning on joining me then; meanwhile, she would be seeing Martin.

When she arrived in the mountains I felt a strange, exhilarating excitement which I thought had come from having gotten closer to the kind of independence we both wanted. But I ignored the panic trickling into my gut, and how hard it was to be away from Ruth's side that whole weekend.

The next morning Gary and I went for a walk. It was very cold and the air felt thin and fresh. There was a thin, crunchy layer of ice on top of the deep-piled snow, but some of the mountain streams were still rushing down the hillsides. The sky was pale blue, and the ice coating the bare branches glistened silver in the morning sun. I talked a blue streak, laying out all the alternatives, all the possible directions I could envision events taking.

"I don't get any sense from you that you're really unsure of what's going to happen," Gary said.

"I am," I said jauntily. "Completely unsure."

"What I'm trying to say," he persisted, "is that I don't have a sense from you that you might eventually need help or need to feel more dependent on Ruth."

"I probably will," I answered; but I didn't understand why he was trying to bring me down.

Gary thought that I was dismissing his warning, he heard me not letting my doubts break through the smooth persuasive surface of my words.

When we got back to Philadelphia Ruth began to spend about a night a week with Martin at his place, always asking me first if it was okay. My nervousness began to increase. For one thing I had been spending time for months with a woman with whom I wasn't sleeping, and I felt competitively one-down. For another, back in the city, I was being exposed to more of Ruth's and Martin's affair. One morning I was still in bed, half-awake, while Ruth was moving around the room getting ready to leave for work. She was packing overnight stuff into a large, red pocketbook be cause she was going directly from the hospital to Martin's house. I saw her put her toothbrush in the bag.

I got out of bed knowing that more than anything I wanted to get laid. I went to a woman whom I had sensed was available, and after a terrible, false, alienating day we went to bed. Afterward, I couldn't find my glasses. I got panicky. By the time I left her I was frantically angry at myself.

After dinner Gary and I went upstairs to my room and I told him what had happened. I said that I didn't want Ruth to spend the night with Martin, that I was finding the whole arrangement hard to bear. Gary and I talked for hours, and in the end I telephoned Ruth and asked her to come home. I could hear that she was powerfully resentful, but also that she was worried about me. The drive back to the house took her away from the excitement of a new romance toward the familiar interdependency of our life together. She was enjoying herself with Martin, it was carefree. Now she knew she was heading toward a morass of my fears, my insecurities, the maturity of our caring. When she got to our room I told her that I wanted her to stop seeing Martin, and that I wouldn't see anybody else either. Ruth wasn't sure, though, that she was ready to return to the kind of protected, exclusive relationship we had. She was getting a sense of herself as her own person which was gratifyingly strong. She didn't intend to let me run her life. She knew that–I would try to pull her in very tight to help heal my wounds.

We both got quite desperate. Ruth screamed, "What's me and what's you? Sometimes I think there's no me, only an us."

122

During that night and the days that followed she was asking herself to what extent she could make her own decisions, how freely she could move outside the marriage whether or not she slept with other men. She was more confident in herself than ever before: finding out in the training program that she wanted to be a therapist gave her a sense of purpose. That sense of becoming herself at last was as close to a feeling of liberation from her past as anything she had ever experienced. Meanwhile, though, she had to decide whether she thought what I wanted was reasonable; she was furious that I was so demanding. Our involvement was so long-standing, so complex. She had to decide on her own limits, on what only she could decide for herself and what she would allow me to decide with her. After a few weeks *she* decided that we could forbid one another to have affairs, and since that was what I wanted too, we reset those limits. But she had learned that she sacrificed as much and as surely as I did by agreeing to a monogamous marriage. And the whole question of what it meant for her to redefine herself remained unanswered.

The next few months were like an emotional steambath. Ruth had been right. I was trying to keep from drowning in hurt and wounded self-respect, and we both had trouble breathing freely. We drew very close together, but there was a deep unresolved mutual antagonism.

I was sleeping restlessly and dreaming every night. A dream: I was in a sterile, white hospital room with Martin, who had just finished fucking Ruth. The shade was up and there was sunlight in the room and a hospital bed with white sheets. Otherwise, the room was empty. I was hitting Martin on the back of the head and shoulder with a rubber truncheon, but completely ineffectually. I left the room and went through the corridor to the next room. It was identical, but the shade was drawn and so the room was dim and gloomy. Ruth was on her back in bed with her red flannel nightgown drawn up around her waist and her legs in the air. A very substantial, tanned, swarthy man in his fifties was just entering her. I could see, in closeup, the look of pleasure on her face as she received him. I began to hit him with my truncheon, also without effect. He turned around and quite effortlessly pushed me back out of the way. Then he entered Ruth again and I watched the pleasure on her face as they began to move in unison . . .

I woke up curled over, almost fetally, with a pain in my gut. It was just before dawn, and I was howling, gnashing the blankets with my teeth. All the pain, accumulated at that moment, broke through feeling into a crystallized thought: the only way through the pain was into myself, there was no avoiding it, no going around. There was so much to understand about myself, so much past jarred loose from the slumbering recesses of my consciousness. That morning, for the first time, I began to understand that the outcome wasn't in Ruth's control. If she never fucked Martin again I might have gained a sanctuary but neither greater acceptance nor increased understanding of myself. I had to give myself more. It was frightening how in a moment so much pain and uncertainty could sweep over me, so completely beyond my control. I felt in so deep, so far beyond where I expected to be. But I also thought that I was strong enough to get back to solid ground. And the truth was that I wanted to grow with Ruth on my terms, and while I knew that she and I would make it through those hard times, I also knew that I was going to have to relinquish some control. Still, though, I clung.

It was important for us to be living in the house in January and February. We were alone to fight or to love when we had to be, but we were also surrounded by caring friends who put out for us because that was the bargain we had struck, because we were all reaping the dividends. Gary told me, "You have a way of describing your dependence on Ruth so strongly it seems as though all she can do is give you what you want. One of the most difficult things for you is to give up control in a way that's not itself very controlling."

And Ruth thought that the experience of living in the house had enlarged her capacity for self-acceptance. "I am the way I am," she told me. "Some of that I like, some I dislike, some I just accept. I've put myself down for feeling needs not generally accepted in the group, but I've always felt accepted in the house. People here have disagreed with me, or tried to change my mind, but nobody's ever said 'That's ridiculous, nobody should feel like that.'"

Sexuality

We had a house meeting at which we didn't talk. We began by breathing and moving in relaxing ways, and then we arranged ourselves in a circle with everybody standing up and facing the center. Ruth strolled contemplatively into the circle. She finally approached Gary, took both of his big hands in her small ones and drew them away from his sides so that they extended forward from his torso. She took two strides away from his outstretched hands, turned her back to him and smiled over her left shoulder, and then fell backward, only his long arms between her and the floor. A leap of faith! Gary caught her, grunting at the impact, and he held her close for a moment before they separated and he entered the circle. He stayed close to the middle, turning. He faced Leigh, towering above her, nearly a full foot taller. As he stepped toward her, his muscles turned to sawdust; like a jointless rag doll he fell. He tried to get up and face her but every time their eyes met he crumbled again. Leigh was laughing, flushed. She entered the circle, went directly to Pete and pulled him down onto the floor where she cradled him in her arms. Later Dan hugged Pete, too. After awhile we piled up together on the floor, writhing, touching, laughing, moving in a confusion of torsos, faces, limbs, hair. In the end we lay quietly entwined, breathing deeply.

There was a more intense sexuality in the house than there had been before. Anne had trouble touching Dan, playing around with him, because she was so excited by the meeting of their bodies. Pete was lonely, an affair had recently ended.

One afternoon Anne and I were sitting on her bed, talking. "I have a certain curiosity about sleeping with Pete," she said. "You know there are all these women filing in and out of his room. Something must be going on in there that I'd like to get in on." She laughed. "But I couldn't handle it."

"Anne, you say that about everything," I chided her.

"That's not true," she pouted.

One night Matt's friend Donna slept over and the two of them decided to take a bath. Ruth and I were sitting in the living room with Pete, Leigh, and Anne. Ruth wanted me to tell them to get out of the bathtub, but I wouldn't.

"I'm not bothered by them taking a bath together," I said. "If you are, you get them out." We were at the edge of our morass again.

Pete asked Ruth, "Why don't you want them to bathe together?" That began a talk about our earliest sexual encounters, about what we had all been taught about sex as children, and what we had learned on our own. Ruth and I managed to avoid a fight in which our feelings about our own and one another's sexuality might well have become hopelessly confused with our desire to do what we thought was best for Matt. While we grownups yakked, the kids finished their bath and went upstairs to play.

Pete and Leigh were developing a special friendship, a surprise to them both. Pete found that he could confide in Leigh. One night while they were sitting together on Leigh's bed she got up in the middle of the conversation and closed the door because she was being distracted by people moving through the hall and wanted more privacy. Pete felt his innards lurch, a lot of the affection he felt for Leigh flooded over him then in a rush of desire. It was all he could do not to jump up and throw her down on the bed. They didn't talk about it.

Meanwhile, the hug which Dan had given Pete at the house meeting seemed to cement their growing good feelings for each other. Pete admired Dan's competence, the way he could fix cars and other machines and farm the land, and was trusting of the younger man's kindness. He also felt a kinship because of the slow, untalkative way they both approached life, both of them content to let events and emotions play themselves out.

A mood, an anticipation, had been emerging between Leigh and Pete. They wanted each other. And Dan, Dan is such an adventurer, is so naturally open and curious. On a cold, clear Sunday afternoon the three of them were sitting quietly in the living room as the sun, dipping toward the west, began to cast a latticework of light and shadow upon the room, bathing it with a drowsy, sensual warmth. They were acutely aware of each other, of the desire and uncertainty in the room. Leigh wanted to make love. She and Dan were snuggled together in the soft, pale green chair, but she was thinking about Pete who was on the couch picking out aimless melodies on his guitar. Pete sensed Leigh's desire but in the languorous, sun-streaked living room he worried that he might be imagining she wanted him because of how badly he desired her. He put down the guitar and went upstairs and sat on his bed. Alone. His fantasies running unbridled.

Soon Dan and Leigh came upstairs to her room and built a fire. But Leigh was still thinking about Pete. Finally she asked Dan if he would mind if Pete joined them and they all gave each other back rubs. It wasn't precisely what she wanted, but it came as close as she was willing to admit. And Dan believed that sex among people who cared about one another should be free and open and uncomplicated. His spirit was open to whatever felt natural and right.

And so finally the three of them were together on the thick red carpet in front of the fire, rubbing each other's bodies with oil, making love. Leigh was the focus, the center of the wondrous sexual tension which communicated itself among them. The two men moved about her, limbs brushing, bodily aware of each other, more physically intimate than either had ever before been with another man. The sun was pouring in through the west window now, saturating the room and the three people in it. Thoughts spinning, bodies moving, a conjunction of rhythms, anticipation finding expression.

Afterward they sat huddled together gazing into the fire, wondering at this new moment. None of them talked about the next day and the next night and what they might bring. Pete was nervous, uncertain; Dan was phlegmatic, satisfied. Something unique among them had been consummated. There was a bond now, a variety of loves and trusts had been exchanged.

The next morning Dan went ahead with his plans to visit his folks for a few days. Pete and Leigh shared a bed the two nights that he was away, but when Dan returned it wasn't so easy.

Leigh would think, "I'd like to be with Pete tonight, but should I be while Dan's in the house?" Many nights she would sleep alone to avoid making a choice, to take the pressure off. It upset her to be feeling more attracted to Pete than to Dan, it felt to her like a desertion, an infidelity. And Pete was not easily able to make love with Leigh if Dan was home. All three of them tried to avoid making any demands on one another because none of them thought that they had the right: there was an almost polite warmth among them.

Meanwhile, as Leigh and Pete (but not Dan) started to talk within the house about what was happening, the rest of us were reacting, there was a certain excitement in the house, fantasies abounded. Anne was jealous of Leigh for sleeping with two men whom she wanted but couldn't have. And late one night she charged into Pete's room and told him that she was feeling square, jealous, out of it. Gary dropped in, too. "Look, you sonofabitch," he said with a half-smile, "you cause me lots of problems bringing these things up in my life."

"Yeah," Pete said. "You know, if I keep getting involved with women who have strong ties to other men there are always bridges that remain uncrossed . . .

"My relationship with Leigh," he continued, musingly. "We've spent a lot of time together out of bed. I really care for her . . . it's something that approaches love."

"I wonder if Leigh is using you to help work out the problems she has with Dan?" Gary asked, and he was disappointed with himself for having asked Pete, but not Leigh.

Ruth was angry and talked about it at a house meeting.

"I felt there was an explicit agreement there wouldn't be any sexual liaisons outside the couples," she said. "That was a rule I was working by." It was a painful time for her to have to incorporate Leigh's bedding down with two men. And she had wanted to sleep with Pete herself the previous fall, when it might have been possible except for the agreed-upon prohibition in the house. She felt that she had been hoodwinked, as if the three of them had not respected an agreement which she had honored.

Leigh was happy making love with Pete, she was more relaxed than she had ever been with a man. But at the same time the burden of two men's feelings was becoming a strain. Dan seemed to her to need a lot of reassurance, but said very little about it; it appeared that he felt obligated to be okay because this situation was something he had wanted. Gradually, Leigh became aware that a choice would have to be made. Pete was beginning to invest himself in her, he dreamt that she bore his child. She was drawn to Pete because of how easy it was for them to talk and love, because he was sure of himself and the direction of his life. But she knew that in the final balance it was Dan whom she wanted to be her man, not Pete.

The two men had continued their warm, untalkative friendship, getting along in a casual way—but the three of them had not been together again. Finally, though, they sat down to talk. Pete was worried that Dan was hurting; but he worried, too, that in the end he would be hurt and alone, left outside their more durable bond.

"How do you feel, Dan?" he asked.

"Okay," Dan said.

"Are you sure?"

"Oh well, I can live with it," Dan said.

Pete began to understand that Dan wasn't going to bare himself to him, so he left Dan and Leigh alone, withdrew. Dan was able to cry then, and holding him, Leigh felt his pain—she had wanted to deny its existence so that she could feel free to go on being with Pete, too, but now that was no longer possible.

The next morning she talked with Pete and they agreed not to go to bed for awhile at least. As it turned out they never made love again. But their intimacy endured. As they eased oil, they were disappointed but relieved.

Perhaps Chris felt more longing and less certainty after the three of them slept together than any of the rest of us. We heterosexuals could at least feel comfortable because our desires were acceptable to each other, we could, without too much cost, talk pretty freely among ourselves about our sexuality. But Chris, uncertain of the others' feelings, especially the men's, and perhaps untrusting of his own desires as well, was forced to squelch his sexuality.

In addition to being the only homosexual in the group, Chris was also the most physically demonstrative person in the house. He would hug you for any good reason, and sometimes for no reason at all. One day, for instance, Ruth came home from the hospital really bushed; she had been feeling alienated from Chris, too, thinking that she had hurt his feelings by being unavailable to him during much of the winter. When she walked in the front door Chris jumped up off the living room couch and headed for her, the glint of a hug apparent in his eye. Ruth said, "Chris, I don't want to hug you now." Chris stopped, turned aside toward the breakfront and sifted through the mail. "Okay," he said sulkily, wondering why the hell she had to make such a big deal of a hug.

At the next house meeting Ruth recalled the incident. "It took a lot for me to be able to say that to you," she told him. "I felt like you received it as a rejection of you. I'm worried that it was a gesture which said more than I intended, but not precisely what I had in mind. Sometimes," she continued hesitantly, seriously, "when you head toward me to hug me like that I sense huge needs in you, I feel like I could almost be gobbled up. That's why I draw back."

"I know what Ruth means," Leigh said quickly, taking the opportunity Ruth had created to say what she had long thought. "Sometimes when you hug me, I feel like I'm on a testing grounds. It doesn't give room for the other person, it really puts me on the spot because it puts me in the position of rejecting something so simple and affectionate as a hug. Every time that's happened I felt a combination of wanting to push you away and guilt for not being able to respond in kind."

"It seems to me," Chris said, hurt, "that you both put more thought in to it than me, when I'm happy to see somebody, I hug them." The way in which Chris said this invited further discussion. Whereas I might have said, "You people are putting too much thought into your hugs," in a brusque way which discouraged any more talk about it, Chris' pouty, self-doubting style had the opposite effect.

"Sometimes I get the feeling that it's almost as if you're seeking reassurance that I care for you," Leigh persisted.

"I just have a need for physical contact with people," Chris said. "There are times when I feel so isolated from certain people that it gets to feeling really terrible."

"Do you feel that way about me?" Leigh asked.

"Not usually," Chris said.

I wondered how many of the others were certain, as I was, that Chris was talking about them.

"When I don't feel like hugging you I feel like my body space is being invaded," Anne said irritably. "Like some times I'm angry and get greeted by a hug and it's almost as though you know I'm angry and want to short-circuit it." She knew that she swallowed more of her annoyance with Chris than with anybody else. Then, all at once, it came pouring out.

"Chris," Leigh said, "sometimes I feel as though the physical contact between us, the hugs and stuff, are the way you express your sexual feelings with women. They're sort of a way you can have physical contact while being safe because you're gay."

"I don't know. Maybe," Chris said, seeming flustered. "I certainly do have sexual feelings toward women, but I don't know what to do with them."

Often Chris would rest his head in the lap of one of the three women, or give a back rub, touching them with an intimacy that would be considered sexual if I or one of the other men were to do it. The muted sexuality of those scenes had always made me uncomfortable.

132

Chris was in high school when he first became sexually involved with other boys, some of them black. By day he was a normal, if somewhat studious and lonely kid. By night, he began to be active in ways that were nearly unimaginable in a town the size of Beaver Falls. When he went away to college at Oberlin in Ohio Chris resolved to turn straight, to try and stay away from men lovers and make it with women. For nearly a year he didn't have sex with a man–nor with a Woman, although he tried. It was a difficult time for him, one which was not true to the messages of his senses. By the end of his second year of college he was acknowledging that he was a homosexual. In the last several years he had felt by and large accepted in his world, but he was seldom at his ease with outspoken, assertive and seemingly callous straight men, who, like me, reminded him of the rough edge of his father's anger. He had been a lonely child who had never felt close to his father. Once, when his mother had returned home after being hospitalized for a nervous breakdown, his father had yelled at her: "Don'.t step out of line with me. All I've got to do is sign a piece of paper and back in you go." And Chris had felt destroyed; he had thought that he would never allow himself to have feelings like his father's, never allow himself to threaten or bully other people.

The tension between Chris and me grew with an arithmetic certainty: incidents, impasses, silences compounding each other. Gary came to talk to me about my high-handed ways with Chris, saying that I was negating him, that I should try to make things better between us. I acknowledged the accuracy of Gary's description, but stubbornly resisted any commitment to a greater effort. Gary, as the messenger of sensible, admirable conduct, was a Gary for whom I had the most meager tolerance.

The next Monday night, although he was apprehensive that I would feel attacked by his saying anything at all, Chris spoke up at the house meeting.

"I've really been having a lot of trouble with you, Mike, lately, and I haven't been able to talk about it." He spoke rapidly, nervously. "I really think that sometimes you talk a lot about support, but the way you come on with me makes me think you don't consider my feelings. Like the day last week when you stepped on the thorns from the rosebushes I had pruned and you came and yelled at me. I got the feeling that I wasn't supposed to say anything, that you weren't interested in my response, and it made me feel you don't respect me as an individual."

"I guess I might come on with a kid that same way," I answered softly. Chris' loneliness depressed me, it was too close to my own fears of an aimless life, I wanted to shout at him: "Keep away from me!" But I didn't. "Maybe I treat you that way because your being gay threatens me, and by treating you like a child I don't have to take you completely seriously. I don't know." I wanted to cry, or evaporate. I was sad and lonely and dispirited.

"Well, it's very hard to bring up, it's a taboo subject," Chris said more confidently, relieved that I had responded without getting angry.

"I think I do value you as a person," I said, wondering whether I really did. I was putting so much effort into being not only receptive to Chris, but non-threatening, honest up to a point, and yet . . . I really didn't know whether I wanted to be having this conversation, or whether my will was being submerged in what I thought the house expected of me. Perhaps I was growing, perhaps I was being diminished.

"There have been times," Leigh said to me, "when I thought you were completely negating Chris. Like once you sort of threw off at a house meeting, 'Of course, Chris and I don't have a relationship.' You said it with a lack of emotion but very strongly, and I felt really bad about myself that I didn't say at the time, 'What the fuck are you saying?'" Leigh detested the cruel way she thought I handled Chris.

"I guess I feel more threatened by your criticism than I'd like to," Anne said to me. "I think you're the strongest personality in the house, and I have no defenses against your anger. But you make an effort to listen to me when I fight back, which you don't do for Chris."

"Chris," Gary said, "I'd like to know more of what you meant when you said your being gay was taboo. At times I've felt a real lack of understanding of your feelings. In addition to my anxiety, I also sensed that it was hard for you to talk about. Maybe that's some of what affects Mike, that it remains so mysterious."

"I guess I've talked to Anne the most about it, and to Leigh some," Chris said. "The women seem less threatening.

"I've spent the last twelve or fourteen years of my life hearing people say that things I'm involved in are ugly," he continued. "I'm always getting the impression that to talk about it is going to turn people off; and I know it's a problem for Mike. There's a whole side of my life, a whole need, which can't be fulfilled in the house. All the rest of you have that option, everybody else has another person here with whom they have, or have had, a sexual relation ship."

I was recalling the talk we had had in Upper Darby when Chris asked if we trusted him with Matt, and how much sympathetic anger and sadness I had felt then. Now I saw that the way I acted fed Chris' doubts about himself, that my sympathies and my actions were operating at cross purposes, and not only didn't I know whether I could change that, I wasn't sure I wanted to try very hard.

"The way things are set up in Philadelphia," Chris said, "I have to relate to people as bodies. There really aren't many places where gay people can mix freely, the only places are really the gay bars."

My political sense grasped the truth of what Chris was saying, but some implacable part of my will rejected the ease with which Chris assigned his problems to his milieu.

"It's really hard to meet people under relaxed circumstances," Chris continued. "When a girl meets a guy I think the possibility that he might be sexually attracted to her isn't shocking. But in the situations where I've been attracted to a guy it's really hard for me to bring it up because I'm worried he might be straight and I'm going to freak him out.

"And a lot of gay people feel uncomfortable being around straight people, which sometimes makes it hard to bring somebody home," he explained, apparently relieved to be able to talk this openly about the problems he lived with as a gay man, the problems of his nighttime world. "I make a distinction between people I'll bring home and people I'll go home with. In gay encounters things tend to move pretty fast, it's kind of shoot first and ask questions later, and I don't want to bring home some unknown quantity, I don't want to feel as though I've inflicted somebody on you all."

"Sometimes when I bring a woman home I feel self conscious, like people are observing," Pete said understandingly.

"You know," Leigh said, "I think we all have homosexual feelings if we let ourselves. I find myself being very attracted to women, I fantasize gay relationships. I haven't acted on those feelings, but I feel less and less as though it's something I can't do. About eighteen months ago I realized I had never allowed myself to fantasize sexual relationships with women, and since then I've let myself explore those things in my own head. I know I'm attracted to Anne, and to Ruth."

*   *   *

It felt to me as though Chris and Dan were gradually being banished from the group. Both men were physical in a way which communicated sexually; Chris in his delicate, finger-probing, tongue and hair raunchiness; and Dan in his muscular awareness and alertness. Their sensuality may have been too great a threat to our social order, to the covenants of restraint among us. Our household was powered by talk, by intellectualization—and by a suppression of sensuality. Dan indicated vaguely from time to time that he hoped sexual barriers would break down in the house, and I think that he really wanted that to happen much more than he let on. For Chris to have been more fully equal he would have had to fuck somebody in the house, which would have meant either his having an affair with a woman, or one of the men participating in homosexual sex. Neither possibility was acceptable.

The tribal compacts among us would have been seriously violated if we had acted upon the sexual possibilities which were desired by Dan and Chris. It was easier to isolate them, and flay them with words and ideas.

Women

There was the hope among Ruth, Leigh, and Anne, all of whom regarded themselves as feminists, that one of the pleasures of living together would be egalitarian, womanly bonds.

In June, 1970, when Leigh and Ruth first met, Leigh was on the verge of quitting after two years of often frustrating but instructive work at a state mental hospital. Although she had participated in the anti-war movement in college, it was at the hospital that she began to think the war was symptomatic of some malady which infected the entire body of American life. The apparently purposeful barbarity of the war in Southeast Asia had at first disenchanted, then dismayed, and finally outraged her; it had given her thinking a political dimension and influenced her decision to begin working with groups organizing against American health institutions. Initially she was dissatisfied there because she felt her work was in vain: as soon as a patient with whom he was working felt confident enough to venture another try he was returned to the same family situation in which his problems had been bred. More often than not it was just a matter of time before the person was returned to the hospital. But as she began to read feminist literature like *Notes From the First Year* and works by such therapists as Szasz and Laing her discomfort became more consciously political. She began to notice that despite the anti hierarchical intentions of the unit where she worked, the aides, most of whom were black, seldom spoke up at "team" meetings, that the patients were never consulted about decisions which affected their lives, and that the women patients were treated even more shoddily than the men. The more she saw was wrong, the more powerless she felt. Her dissatisfaction and distress were similar to mine as a newspaper reporter: she did not think her work was dishonorable, but because she was employed by an institution and limited by its strictures she felt implicated in the kind of subtle but relentless harm it was doing. Her feeling of powerlessness now extended beyond the war and into the place where she worked. After awhile the only alternative that made any sense to her began with the belief that the masses of people who suffered the indifference of the American power conglomerate could and should organize to seize power. And so she left the hospital and helped to organize Health Information Project, a collective that worked with neighborhood and worker groups lighting for a greater share of power.

Leigh and Ruth both drove to Chicago in July, 1970, to participate in a protest action against the American Medical Association at its convention. Ruth was working on the staff of the Medical Committee for Human Rights, a left-wing alternative to the AMA, and for the first time was being exposed to feminist thinking. For her, the weekend in Chicago turned out to be epochal. During a speech by a man opposing abortion reform, she wrestled with him for the microphone–she had never believed that she possessed a capacity for physical aggression–and finally triumphant, made a passionate, personal speech amid an uproar surrounding the battle for control of the podium.

"I have lived through an unwanted pregnancy," she said, her voice clotted by rage, incipient tears, and the painful point of understanding. "I can't change that and I have a wonderful son. But if I can help it, no woman will ever have to live through what I did if she doesn't want to. We are not a minority. We are fifty-one percent of the population of this country, and we are not asking for abortions to be freely available to whoever wants them. We're just going to take what we want and nothing will stop us."

The two women liked each other at once.

Leigh was drawn to Ruth's quiet self-containment, but also to the strength and confidence with which she spoke when she was ready. Leigh thought of herself as being something of a magpie, and she wanted to grow into the kind of self-possessed maturity which Ruth seemed to have. She liked Ruth's soft, serious face, her long, reddish brown hair, even the Indian print pants-jumper she was wearing that weekend.

The next time they met was at a party in Philadelphia. Ruth, who was unwilling to go without a bathing suit, felt a stab of jealousy watching Leigh among the volleyball players who were splashing around in a pool unselfconsciously naked; Leigh had a lovely, delicate body which Ruth envied and about which she imagined Leigh could have no misgivings. She had hardly noticed Leigh's slight limp. That fall Leigh joined Ruth's consciousness raising group, and as Ruth got to know her better she came to admire her mental toughness–a gutsy, stubborn resolve. Ruth wished that she had more of Leigh's determination to go after and get what she wanted. And Leigh had retained a freedom to choose: would she have children or not? would she marry or remain independent of any one man? Ruth, meanwhile, was wed to me and to Matt–at a very young age the shape of her life had been determined by forces outside her control, she felt. Leigh was seizing control of her own life in a way Ruth regretted not having done. She had maintained her autonomy in the years after Matt's birth by believing that if she did what was right for herself it would also be best for him. She thought it was a mistake to shape her life according to some notion of what a parent should be like, she didn't want to find herself saying to her son, "Look at all I've sacrificed for you." In this she had an invaluable legacy bestowed on her by her mother, a practicing lawyer who had always let her daughter know that she was important to her while maintaining an active life of her own.

In the women's group, Leigh felt separated from Ruth because she was a mother and a wife–she didn't know whether there was anything she could offer the older woman. And her uncertainty stiffened almost into distrust just before we moved to Cliveden street when Ruth and I said that we didn't want to live with a group of people who were all several years younger than we were. Leigh was sure that despite her admiration for Ruth, Ruth didn't respect her for what she had to offer. But Ruth wanted Leigh to understand that although she valued their friend ship she needed the reassurance of living with some other people whose lives had been more like her own. She didn't know how to make Leigh understand that when she had been twenty-four she had been unhappily married, working as an assistant buyer in a department store, and eating diet pills to keep herself going. She had felt washed up before her life had really begun; now she felt that she couldn't explain to Leigh what it had been like when she had finally cracked up, had fallen apart, and then begun the arduous job of remaking herself. She was frustrated by her inability to express how hard she had worked to reclaim her sense of worth and self-liking over the years. She had floated very loose for a year or two after we left Baltimore, and by the time we were talking to Dan and Leigh about a new house Ruth wanted a kind of security which, though she suspected it might be spurious, had meaning for her.

When Ruth and I suggested that we might want to ask Gary and Anne to live with us, Leigh decided in a flash that Ruth and Anne would get together and she would be on the outside.

And, indeed, Ruth and Anne did have a rapport. When Anne was trying to decide whether or not to move into the house, it was Ruth to whom she talked about her doubts and misgivings, Ruth whom she instinctively trusted. Anne, whose commitment to people once made was ferocious and enduring, decided that she and Ruth could be very, very close. And Ruth responded enthusiastically; she sensed something solid and unshakable about Anne, a firmness about the way she spoke and acted. She thought Anne was beautiful. There was, they both acknowledged after awhile, a feeling of mothering to what they offered one another, the distances between them were alive with the intensity of what they wanted.

Meanwhile, Anne and Leigh moved cautiously to explore each other's psychic terrain, each wary that she would be the odd woman out. Anne's fantasy was that she and Gary would retire to their room while the rest of us had fun together. She was intimidated by Leigh's sweet prettiness, her wide-open blue-gray eyes which seemed to take in what was going on; she was sure that she wouldn't measure up to the standards of this independent woman.

At first Leigh thought that Anne was too straight, too desirous of privacy. But as they spent more time together she learned that Anne's values were similar to hers, although she was still uncertain how deeply Anne incorporated what she believed into how she lived.

*   *   *

During the fervor of our first month in the house Leigh watched as Ruth engaged Dan, trying to fight through the feeling of being outside his life. Seeing Ruth joust with him over the same kinds of distances which separated her from Dan, Leigh was encouraged to think that she and Ruth would be able to overcome their insecurities about each other. But an incident in mid-October caused enough hurt to drive them much farther apart.

One Saturday morning Ruth was depressed and asked Anne to come up to our room where they sat alone and talked. Ruth began to cry, and to tell Anne about her pregnancy and its aftermath, about her dislike for her own body. She found that she was able to give herself up to her own despair and loneliness with Anne, found that she could talk to her about pain it was even hard to think about. Leigh, meanwhile, was prowling around the house, feeling left out; She desperately wanted to be included, imagined that the other two women were talking about her, perhaps even laughing at her—in the absence of knowledge her imaginings were powered by her own doubts and fears. She had heard just enough before they went upstairs to know that they were talking about their bodies. She felt deprived of her right to her doubts about her own body—what did they know about the trouble her hip gave her when she made love, how awkward she felt, how at times all through her life she had felt little better than a cripple? Could they know that as a child who wore a hip brace she had a recurring nightmare of being strafed by an attacking plane while all the healthy-limbed children ran to safety? She wanted to share her feelings with Ruth and Anne, not to feel bitterly excluded by them. Finally she decided to knock at the door and tell them what she was thinking and fearing. The knock startled Ruth, deep in her own sorrow. Leigh opened the door a bit and peered in. The two women had been crying and were sitting pressed together on the bed. Ruth was aware of not asking Leigh to stay. Leigh thought that Ruth asked her to leave; Ruth thought that Anne had. But no matter who had spoken up, Leigh knew she wasn't wanted, and so withdrew and closed the door again. She was shocked, resentful, hurt that the other two women didn't want her. She went across the hall into her own room and cried by herself. Later, Anne came in and comforted her, and Leigh told Anne how devastated she felt. But when Ruth came in too Leigh didn't know how to react. She knew that Ruth was trying to make amends, but she didn't feel receptive. And she didn't let herself cry in front of Ruth, didn't let herself appear Weak and sad. It was months and months before they spoke to each other about that morning.

By November Ruth was withdrawing more and more into her new job and herself. She would come home from work and collapse in our room. Very often Matt and I were the only people whose company she welcomed. Though every body in the house sympathized with her exhaustion, and subsequently with her preoccupation with the aftermath of her affair with Martin, they were also hurt by how little she offered them. Leigh felt excluded from Ruth's confidence when Ruth was feeling weak, or trapped, or sapped of her own resources, and so she had never experienced Ruth offering her the respect of reliance. Though they remained friendly, and often had fun together, they avoided talking in any depth about their relationship. But later in the winter Ruth found it easy to talk to Leigh about wanting to be more independent, and about Martin and me, perhaps because she respected Leigh's insistence on her right to be and do as she pleased. Leigh grudgingly acknowledged to herself that Ruth had her vulnerabilities, too.

Anne was at first puzzled and then hurt and angered when Ruth withdrew. She thought that Ruth was not living up to her responsibilities. She got bugged when Ruth started to avoid doing her house job, but Ruth seemed to be so beset by her own problems and sadness it was just about impossible to be critical of her. Anne showed her disapproval in an occasional sullen suspension of good feelings, a judgmental closing up.

With Ruth so tied up in herself, Leigh and Anne were discovering how much they genuinely liked one another. I thought that Leigh might also be taking a private, jealous pleasure in supplanting Ruth in Anne's confidence. Perhaps she thought that for a change it was Ruth who felt left out.

Each weekday morning Anne and Leigh would leave the house together, get into the VW or the Toyota, light up cigarettes, and talk as they drove down the east bank of the Wissahickon Creek, crossed the Schuylkill River at the Falls Bridge, and then continued down the river's west bank dappled with morning sunlight and shade from the stately trees. In that half-hour they spent together driving to work the two women created an isolated, intimate world all their own. There was no especially memorable incident, no climax, just a relaxed clowning around on some days, and more purposeful talk on others.

Almost at once they began to talk about their mothers. Leigh recalled almost nothing of her natural mother, who left home when she was less than three, but she told Anne about her first stepmother dragging her around by the hair until she began to run away from home, about how the woman became an alcoholic and eventually showed Leigh snapshots of her father and a house guest undressed and in various poses together.

"I began to call her 'mother' just before they separated when I was eleven," Leigh said to Anne, "Not mom, mother."

Leigh made Anne feel protective, as if the younger woman were a sister. Listening to Leigh talk about the unhappiness of

144

that part of her childhood reminded Anne of her own mother's illness when she was five years old, triggered memories of panic and feeling left out, of how, puzzled by her mother's inexplicable behavior, she screamed and yelled and got a reputation as a problem kid, a hell raiser.

Anne was aware of the differences in age and experience which existed between the two of them, but she grew to appreciate Leigh's sympathetic honesty, learned that Leigh would be straight with her. Anne liked Leigh for never giving her comfort while withholding criticism, she appreciated that respect. Her respect for Leigh grew and grew. Anne had always doubted her own intellectual seriousness, like so many women she had been persuaded that her mind wasn't as sharp and resilient and active as a man's. Despite the turmoil of her childhood, Leigh had grown up feeling that she could do anything; her father had encouraged her intellectual efforts, his house was usually full of interesting and stimulating people, and Leigh had always known that she was intellectually competent. Her commitment to political ideas and to her work was sophisticated and intrinsic.

Anne admired Leigh, but she never thought of their friendship as being equal: it seemed to her there were interlocking dependencies, and a competitive edge. On her side was her maturity, her marriage, her fuller sense of having come into herself; on Leigh's was her seriousness about her own mind, her assumption of independence. Anne felt more equal to and less competitive with Ruth, and both of them were uneasy with the ways in which Leigh would sometimes become a kind of child-woman, pouting and pretty and cajoling in order to get her own way. There was a seductive quality to Leigh that made Anne think she was more dependent on a man giving her security than her feminist convictions indicated.

By the time it was clear that Gary and Anne would truly be leaving Ruth had decided to make a new effort with Leigh. For a while, at least, they would probably be the only two women in the house, and Ruth thought it would be awful if they couldn't rely on each other. But she was worried that if she made an overture Leigh might not be receptive. She had made up her mind that Leigh was intimidated by her. She had noticed that although Leigh talked a lot about her father, she seldom said anything about either her natural mother or either of her stepmothers. Ruth suspected that Leigh wasn't ready to untangle the knots of her multimothered motherlessness, and that part of Leigh's attitude in regard to her was more symbolic than personal. Like Anne, Ruth respected Leigh but was also jealous of her. And so, if Leigh reacted less to Ruth's sense of herself than to an idealized image of self-possessed motherhood, Ruth's fantasies of Leigh were no less persuasive. But they pursued their friendship with a dogged faith. They had not happened to each other easily, but they made an unremitting effort to be straight with each other.

In mid-March, Ruth, who was wound up in knots, finally said to Leigh that the time had come to acknowledge the distances and begin to close them. Leigh, every bit as anxious and hopeful, readily agreed.

Anne was relieved. For months she had been watching her step in order not to make Leigh feel jealous or left out, and she was tired of the effort. She wanted to spend more time alone with Ruth. She appreciated the irony of finding herself to be the pivot among the three of them, and not some far-flung spoke after all. How different the year was turning out from what she had expected. When Ruth and Leigh made a date to go out to dinner together Anne was pleased but also sad because it was an acute reminder that she would soon be leaving.

Leigh and Ruth met downtown at a Middle Eastern restaurant where they had a drink, and then another. They ordered two huge, exotic dinners. They talked about their impressions of each other, about Ruth and Martin and me, about Leigh and Pete and Dan. Ruth talked fast, trying to make up for lost time, stumbling over ideas. Her faith was in vomiting up all her accumulated doubts and wishes and grudges and affection, in a baring of herself which she hoped was implicitly saying, Here it all is, now do you accept me? Leigh thought there was something of the feel of a first date to the evening, some awkward anticipation. She was sensitive to the rhythm of what passed between them, to the veering toward each other, and then the nervous hesitation, the looking for where to go next. She felt strained and uncomfortable and, more than that, afraid still that Ruth just didn't give a shit. She despaired a bit. Where would they' go anyway, with all this longing and lunging and retreating?

They drove home late, tipsy and perfumed by all the rich aromas of garlic, cumin, cardamon. In the upstairs hall, before they went to their separate bedrooms, they hugged affectionately. Ruth was happy but Leigh still felt sad, unsatisfied.

Both wanted, alternately, to sweep aside their history, or to run far, far away from each other. For awhile they waited for the climax which never came. But there was a slow accumulation of moments: unexpected ease over coffee in the kitchen late at night, a friendly Saturday morning expedition to a greenhouse, a glance as they shared a private joke. Their mistrust, still not confronted, no longer occupied the foreground of their friendship quite so ominously as it had. But neither was there the kind of resolution which might have come from one unmistakable gesture of sacrifice or risk. And really, it probably would have to come from Leigh because she felt herself to be aggrieved, and so it was she who would have to signal unambiguously that the past was behind her. Ruth could do no more than reassure Leigh of her intentions past and present, could include her no more fully than she had at the restaurant. Leigh's feeling of loss was greater and so her risk in behalf of gain would have to be commensurate.

Meanwhile, winter had begun to relinquish its chill grip on the city. The first promise of spring began to show itself in a morning sun almost warm enough to lure me barefoot onto the still crunchy earth of the backyard. A single white tulip sprouted in front of the house, lonely and fragile and very nearly alien. One unseasonably mild day Leigh spread a blanket out in the backyard and sat there playing her guitar while Anne sunbathed beside her and Ruth hung wash on the line. As Leigh played and sang in her sweet, high voice she regretted that somehow the three of them had never done much together, somehow they had always been in twos.

Decision-making

Spring is the season in which possibilities abound. Like the fleshy white blossoms of the magnolia outside my open window, questions revealed themselves overnight. Our style of looking for answers had assumed an almost ritual familiarity, and we were confident about the way we made decisions, singly and together.

At different times and in certain kinds of situations we had all been influential within the house. I probably talked more than anybody else at house meetings, and the sheer weight and volume of my convictions sometimes gave me an out-sized influence. Leigh and Gary came closest to my style of persuasiveness. All three of us, in addition to being outspoken, continually expressed our interest in the politics of communal living–we were the most likely to talk about lifestyle. Because we speculated more than anybody else, it wasn't unusual for a house meeting to turn on one of our ideas. Pete and Dan had a more limited sphere of influence: either might speak up succinctly and forcefully, but they were adaptable and reacted more often than they initiated. Neither of them was likely to tell the group what he wanted it to do, but both of them did say to the group, "Here's what *I* intend to do." Chris was probably the least influential person in our arrangements because he asked for very little, practically nothing. Anne and Ruth were similar to each other in style, both sometimes took a leading role, but at other times were silent. When Ruth did speak up she was forceful, probably because it cost her such a great effort to make demands. The force either of them could generate, in addition to the respect they both commanded for being level-headed, helped them get what they wanted.

We were all pretty well aware of one another's styles of persuasion, and had fun parodying them. I found it comfortable to be so well seen, so transparently available. I liked myself more after a year on Cliveden street than I had before.

We were usually unconscionably long-winded about the most niggling matters, haggling over details. There was a premium placed on being loose and easy–mellow was a group image we hoped for. But, in fact, the more adamantly somebody wanted something, the more likely they were to get it. When there was disagreement, however, we would spend hours worrying a question until everybody was willing to accept a common answer, and hopefully, be reasonably satisfied with it.

Majority rule, so far as I'm concerned, is a lousy way to make decisions, though it might be a relatively democratic procedure where people can't talk directly one to another. There is no reason except for an utter indifference to individuality, however, for a group of nine to make decisions by vote. Our style of reaching agreements was to talk: our frame of reference, our goals, our assumptions were in the open and had been exhaustively discussed, and so there was very little suspicion about hidden motives.

There were times when an individual brought what would usually be considered a private decision to the group, for instance when Pete asked how the rest of us would feel if he bought a motorcycle with his own money (he was aware that there might be either economic or ecological objections–and there were, but nobody suggested he shouldn't buy the bike). On the other hand, when Ruth and I wanted to have a baby, though ultimately it would effect the lives of the people with whom we were living (Ruth's earnings would stop for awhile, the group's expenses would increase, there would be new responsibilities), we made our decision pretty much on our own and then presented it to the group.

The slipperiest decisions always involved reconciling privacy and communality, the individual and the house. Sometimes the house would intrude into an individual's life: living together made us susceptible to one another's moods. Our group life was animated by spurts of energy mingled with more passive, private cycles. The timing of a problem was essential to our mode of resolving it. At a time of highly charged give and take, we were more likely to insist on responses to group or individual overtures; during slow and easy times there was more patience. I never felt that I was living with a band of great white hunters who were after my head as a trophy. I knew I was liked and respected, and that made me trust that if I submitted myself to some group decisions with which I didn't agree I would still be gaining more from other people's wisdom and understanding than I would be sacrificing in individuality or privacy.

*   *   *

In the spring, after two years of thinking about it, Ruth and I decided to have another child. The winter's desperation had waned, new life was stirring all around us, and we felt sure of ourselves and our future. But we also knew that we never again wanted to raise a child alone and on our own, as we had raised Matt. The isolation of raising a kid in a nuclear family seemed unnecessary, the advantages of having the help and guidance of other adults apparent. And we wanted our second child to have the companionship which Matt had lacked. Gary and Anne were trying to conceive, and Ruth and I were excited by the possibility of raising the two children together. So one mild night the four of us walked through Germantown to a restaurant, and there, over dinner, we decided to move to San Francisco the following summer, when Gary and Anne had settled after their year of travel, and go on living together. On the walk home a brown rabbit with a white tail scurried out of our path and hopped across a lawn into the shadows. A fertility omen, no doubt.

We were excited when we arrived at the house, laughing and talking. Ruth and I sat down and talked with Matt, and he shared our happiness about having a baby–for years he had been suggesting that we provide him with a brother or sister. Then we talked with the adults.I suppose in our own excitement we hadn't given much thought to how the news of our planned move west would strike them. In fact, it had the impact of a ten-ton weight.

Pete seemed dubious about whether we'd follow through. He thought that Ruth and I were in the habit of getting enthusiastic about one idea or another, blowing up our own expectations and those of the people around us, cooling off, and then backing away. Gary and Anne, who had watched us run through that cycle a number of times, didn't say so, but they were also concerned that we wouldn't really follow up, that before the time came to move to California we would have changed our minds. Over the next few weeks they restrained themselves because they were worried about our reliability; Ruth and I, sensing their hesitation but not knowing its source, began to suspect that they really didn't want us to come after all. Gary also had some doubts about making plans a year in advance just when he thought he was learning to take things one at a time, to loosen up the grip of his own drivenness. His desk, for instance, habitually tidy by virtue of always being up to date, was now piled with letters, forms, notes, which had been awhile accumulating, but which he was overlooking because he didn't really want to be doing anything about them. He was pleased about this more relaxed attitude, about not letting his time be cluttered with petty tasks which had always contributed to the overbearing way he could judge and push other people toward performances to meet his standards.

It was Leigh, more than anybody else, who felt left out and torn by divided loyalties, divided affections. Living in the group had made her feel more independent and more self-sufficient than ever before. We had seen her angry, harping, joyful, depressed–in every emotional extreme, in every psychological posture–and we confirmed what she always knew but was afraid to acknowledge to herself: she was not only intelligent, funny, caring, and loyal, but lovable and loving. Loving! Ah, she thought not–in this, though we knew her well, we must be mistaken. Hadn't her parents told her when she was just a girl refereeing their vitriolic fights, hadn't they told her that she was cold and a failure at loving because at the age of fourteen she wanted to escape them and their battles? And hadn't she, after all, let down Adam after their long, sweet, clinging college romance? And didn't that prove it? But in the house she found, especially with Anne and Pete, that her love was received, valued, returned.

At first you might have needed the most sensitive of thermometers to measure her increased warmth, but by degrees it made itself felt. Her desire to share herself with other people was being expressed in more elementary ways than ever before, she was transcending her self characterization. Especially with Anne, never before had she felt such a passion of intimate caring with another woman. And now, as Anne rambled happily on about her plans with Ruth, and Matt, and me–plans from which Leigh was excluded–she became curt, matter-of-fact, hurt. It mattered a great deal to her that we had sat down without any delay and talked to her, she understood the sensitivity of that gesture. But facts were facts. We had made plans which probably wouldn't include her. She wasn't ready to even think about asking if she could come along. First of all there was Dan, and her attachment to him, and his insistence on getting out to the country at the end of his internship. Which presented its own conflict, because she felt tied to Philadelphia. Politically, her ties were to big cities, where, as she saw it, the capitalist system did the most harm and where there was also the greatest hope that it would be eventually toppled. City people needed the most help in organizing themselves. But even more specifically, here in Philadelphia she had poured all her effort and commitment into HIP for two years, and it was just now jelling in the most satisfying ways–and there was also the women's health group. These were political structures she had helped to build because she believed in them, and she wasn't the kind of person who could just walk away from them. But even if she could leave them, there was still Dan. Because some days she wanted to make her plans with him, and some days she didn't. And at that moment all she knew was that she was hurt, and alone, and confused.

$$* \quad * \quad *$$

The weeks rolled on. The rhododendron, the lilac, and the Wisteria bloomed in the backyard, and the bees appeared moving diligently through the pink blossoms of the pear and nectarine trees and among the delicate white flowers of the apple tree. The flowering trees gave promise of fruit, while the strawberry patch grew green and tangled along the ground. Every afternoon Chris worked in the backyard; with Pete, he began to prepare the earth for our vegetable garden, and to put up seeds for carrots, for scallions and greens, for tomatoes, green and red peppers, lettuce and radishes. The seeds were put up in small earthenware pots on the sunny back porch and elsewhere in the house while the black earth was turned and raked and readied. We sprouted seeds from that glorious grass we had smoked the summer before, seeds sent to us specially from California by Anne's Uncle Berle. With a friend I had made ten gallons of beer in our kitchen, which was now aged in bottles and ready for drinking. Pete often baked bread. Along with the care and devotion which so frequently went into the preparation of meals, all these makings and growings were giving me the feeling that we were healthy and sufficient, that we were learning a little bit at a time how to escape the poisons which sometimes seemed to seep through every pore in the avaricious face of our society, in its polluted environment, its adulterated food, its distortion of language, its discriminatory laws, its brutal pursuit of war abroad and calm at home.

It was a time in our lives together when I had every reason to expect that our decisions would be reached amiably and sensibly. Our friendships were, in many in stances, warm and fulfilling, our sentimentality moving toward a peak, our experiences in solving problems solid and confidence-inspiring. And so, with very little effort, we managed to have a donnybrook.

A stray young mutt whom some of us called Clive—and others called Elijah because he arrived on the first day of Passover—had taken to hanging around. He wasn't much to look at and I don't think anybody was really attached to him, some people just sort of felt vaguely responsible for his well-being. Which should not have presented any problems, except that Pete and Leigh had been saying for weeks that they wanted a puppy. They were meeting resistance from nearly everybody else, although the argument had consisted mostly of bantering. Now, Clive—Elijah's arrival caused them to worry that they wouldn't get a chance to raise a puppy, that this mutt would be foisted off on them instead. Both of them thought that they didn't get their own way often enough in our group deliberations, that Gary and I, and Ruth and Anne, were all more willing to push for what we wanted. Pete was trying to discipline himself to speak up more often in his own behalf. He had made it clear he wanted a puppy of his own choosing, and so construed the mutt's presence around the house as a sign that the group was ignoring his wish. Over the course of the year Leigh had become more of an instigator, she had moved steadily toward becoming more and more influential. Near the beginning of the year she too had been told repeatedly that she was too slow in speaking up, in pleading her cause when there was something she wanted. Now what she wanted was a Chesapeake Bay Retriever. It was a Friday evening when Pete saw a newspaper ad for Chesapeake puppies selling at fifty dollars apiece. We were all in our usual slightly hysterical, Friday-night-dinner state when Pete suggested that he and Leigh could drive over to Wilmington that night and pick themselves up a puppy. Whether or not they should became a great contention.

"I don't see why you should buy a puppy when the pound is full of dogs who need a home," Ruth said, her judgement unmistakable.

"Because we want a Chesapeake," Leigh said defensively.

155

"Chesapeake, shmesapeake, what difference does it make?" I asked mockingly.

"Listen," Pete said stubbornly, "we really want a Chesapeake pup."

"Yeah," I replied resentfully, "but if there's a puppy around the house it's going to be everybody's problem until it's housebroken, and I really don't want to take that on."

"Nobody else has to clean up its shit," Pete said. "I'll take all the responsibility for caring for it." He had turned pink in the face, and had a tight, sardonic grin which appeared only when he felt thwarted.

"Aw come on, that's just not realistic," Ruth exclaimed.

There was an exasperated silence while we all went on eating and silently marshaling our arguments.

"Well, I don't know," Dan said contemptuously. "Why spend fifty dollars for a dog when there's plenty of good dogs around free?"

"And if you get a dog from the pound you save its life," Anne added in her best guilt-inducing manner.

After awhile Pete and Leigh got ready to leave. Anne and I, who were by then sitting in the living room bitching to each other, asked them to wait and consider it further, but they were intent. I was angriest not about the puppy, but at the cavalier way they were overriding the objections from the rest of us. Later that night they brought home the Chesapeake puppy, which became the lightning rod for almost any and all anger and tension in the house. For awhile she puked, pissed, shit and teethed all over the house, got disciplined in a bewildering variety of styles, and slinked a lot when she was worried that she had done something wrong, which was most of the time.

I was angry for a long time afterward because of the way Pete and Leigh had decided to buy the puppy despite all the opposition. I suppose I also had some understanding of what had motivated them: they really wanted that dog and knew there was a chance they wouldn't get it if they submitted to the usual give and take of a house meeting. The crunch between independent will and communal preference was no unfamiliar. Living cooperatively meant giving up some freedom to do

156

what you wanted, when you wanted, how you wanted. Of course, in our society people who try to act as if they were truly free wind up in prisons or mental hospitals–maybe some of them land in communes, too. But living in our house made everybody want to tell the group to go take a flying fuck every once in a while. That urge, healthy as it might have been for individuals , was also threatening to the house, and so was seldom expressed fully and spontaneously. We were more likely to be caustic, brittle, mocking, logical, or exasperated than just enraged.

This reserve sometimes made me feel stifled by living in the house. A lot of the real pizzazz in our moments of irrational frustration and anger with one another dribbled off into statement like, "I'm really pissed off because . . ." Very cerebral. All too often we succumbed to the pressure to explain ourselves. People would stifle their strongest feelings because they suspected themselves of being motivated by reasons that were too individualistic, or too middle-class, or too intolerant, or too uncompromising–because they thought that in some way their emotional bursts ran contrary to the notion of correct communal behavior.

Perhaps we could have justified our inhibitions by saying that in order to live communally we needed to be supportive, considerate, and respectful of differences, that we needed to suppress some petty annoyances and irritations. Certainly in that respect communal living doesn't differ from any other social contract, including marriage. But it made me wonder about our tacit rules of conduct, what they were and how they had evolved.

* * *

We had told a lot of our friends that we wanted to meet people with kids who were interested in joining a commune, and before too long we got a call from Linda, a single woman with a five-year-old daughter. Linda said that she was interested in a commune which had the kind of intimacy she was used to in her consciousness raising group. We invited her to visit.

As the day of her visit drew closer and closer our fantasies took flight. We wanted to be careful not to overwhelm her, to give her a chance, but we were also desirous and curious. We wondered whether we would like her, whether she would come to share our lives. Yes, that was it. Would she become one of us? Would she some of the empty spaces when Gary and Anne departed? Finally there was the expected knock. on the door. The atmosphere was a kind of subdued, uncertain agitation.

"Here they are," Leigh yelled from the kitchen up the back stairs. Predictably, as many of us were hiding as not. Leigh and I reached the door about the same time. I pulled it open, ready to greet our future, and there stood—a stranger. She was tall, broad-boned. Her black hair was tied back, and she had an expectant, apprehensive smile. Leigh and I were repeating, "Come in, come in," Ruth was coming down the stairs, the dogs were barking and jumping, Matt appeared out of nowhere bouncing like a rubber ball, and the hysteria level was high as a kite in full sail. The little girl clung to her mother. We began to talk, to stroll around the house and the yard showing Linda the place. I recognized in Leigh's behavior, in Ruth's and in my own a kind of super-reality: we were all recognizable, but a little bigger and better than life— more jovial, more open and warm, more images of ourselves than natural. It would take us awhile to get back down to earth.

Linda seemed likable, but I was still struggling to understand that she was a stranger, that I didn't know her. In my fantasies prior to her coming I had opened the door and there stood a woman whose expression suggested a vast knowledge of me and my way of life, a kind of Good Witch of Communal Living. I was still hurrying to catch up to reality. There was so much to say and so many of us to say it. I tried to consider Linda's situation:

She was sitting in an unfamiliar living room talking with a group of adults she had never met before, she wasn't even certain of all our names. We generated an extraordinary group energy, our conversation was fast-paced, our references sometimes puzzlingly private, our transitions from kidding around to being serious not always apparent especially to somebody who wanted to make a favorable impression. She was aware that she was being measured, assessed, sensed, and she was probably wondering what was expected of her. Meanwhile, she was also trying to decide whether she liked and wanted us. Whatever happened would include her daughter as well as her. She was young, only twenty-three, to have such a heavy, lonely responsibility.

In time, after more visits and more talk, she began to come into focus. I liked her, and so did everybody else. The assumption began to take root, not willfully, that she would probably move in; we were all aware of the growth of this idea, but it was never specifically considered. There were problems, as there would be with anybody. She was diffident, so much so that I thought she asked too much by offering too little. And, though her daughter played nicely with Matt, they were not compatriots; he felt responsible for entertaining her in the way an older brother might.

Then, when we were pondering, we met Jean and her two kids, and a considerable enthusiasm was generated. Her son and Matt were pals at once: eight-year-old pirates terrorizing the house and then sailing away on a sea of triumphant, defiant laughter. Her daughter was loud and brassy and charmed me by asking in a loud, four-year-old voice at dinner: "Do you and Ruth sleep in one bed? Do you dream about each other? Are you in love?" And Jean was outgoing, very physical, she made herself felt. Her entrance into the group was made easier by our experience with Linda, this time we knew enough to expect a stranger, and what we asked of her was probably more realistic and easier to handle. We told both women that Ruth, Matt, and I would probably be moving west in a year.

The time had come to make a decision. But there was much more to this matter than just which of these two families we would ask to live with us. We were close-knit, and when we opened ourselves up many stitches would come unraveled.

Ruth was aggrieved. For months she had been saying that she wanted a room of her own when one was available even if that meant no new people joining the house; and now we were beginning to consider who would move in.

"I've shared a room with Mike for a long, long time," she said, "and I can go on doing that. But I've been craving space of my own–I have no space of my own. My life is really very peopled, you know? I'm not sure that I'm willing to chuck all the psychic space and living space I'd gain when Gary and Anne leave just to have another kid around.

"I feel a great guilt about maybe depriving Matt of other kids. But I want a room of my own." She paused and sighed. "I don't think people have been respecting my needs."

Her urgency was increasing, and Pete felt a familiar envious resentment at Ruth's capacity to say what she wanted with so much conviction that she was entitled to get it. But he said nothing, and mentally kicked himself in the ass for holding back.

Ruth turned to Leigh and said loudly and firmly, "I think you want Linda or Jean to move in because then there'll be another woman in the house and you won't have to put so much energy into me." I knew it cost Ruth considerable pain and doubt to say that.

Gary went, "Ahhhh."

"Sometimes, Leigh," Ruth continued, "I think you try to get your way by being coy or coquettish. All this is hard to say . . . I'm hurt because I don't think you appreciated the kind of confidences I shared with you when we had dinner out, you know? I really put out that night." Her voice faltered, it was raw, taut. "Sometimes I feel like you really don't care about me."

"I'm really confused," Leigh responded at once. She sounded composed, but not detached. She was hunched forward, lighting a cigarette. "What you're describing just isn't me. I do care, but I get the feeling sometimes that when I try to get closer to you, you put me off." Suddenly she was no longer plaintive, but angry. "And that thing about another woman moving in is really off the wall. When Jean was over you sat down with her and Mike and talked for hours about being parents. I guess I thought you were doing that to exclude me, but that felt pretty paranoid. I don't know."

"Jesus Christ," Gary whispered.

"For god's sake, Gary, will you stop making noises every time a thought crosses your mind," I snapped irritably.

"It does kind of set you up as some kind of pontificate," Pete said, "just sitting back there having all these insights."

"And it distracts attention from what's going on," Anne said pointedly.

"Part of where I'm coming from," Ruth resumed, "has to do with the feeling that I'm the only one who's really going to be giving up something important if new people move in–the rest of you will all have rooms of your own. I guess I'm willing to do that because of Matt, but I don't think my objections have been treated with consideration."

I was greatly relieved. I had been stymied by wanting Jean and her kids to move in and knowing that Ruth was entitled to what she wanted.

"I'm really glad you're willing to have other people in," I said. "I really felt caught in between."

"I know that I'm really very wary about any new people," Ruth said. "I tend to put aside my doubts and then they come back to plague me. But I'm willing."

"We haven't been real careful all the way along," Leigh said. "We sort of went whoosh, first with Linda and then with Jean. And people who wanted to slow down were swept along. Mike, you probably did that more than anyone else."

"Yeah, that's true," I acknowledged. "And now that I'm more inclined to live with Jean because of how the kids got along–and because I really hit it off with her–I don't know how to go back to Linda and tell her it's all off. I really contributed to building up her expectations."

"I really got off on how the two boys ran wild," Anne said enthusiastically. "I got in touch with how hard that's been for Matt to do on his own."

"I think I'd prefer to live with Linda," Pete said. "But the sense I'm starting to get is that the group is favoring Jean."

"It's hard," Leigh said. "I like Linda. But I think Matt would be better off with a boy his own age–that was the whole idea of looking for new people. And I like Jean, too."

"I feel awful thinking about Linda," I said.

"It's just really important that if we decide to ask Jean to move in we stick by Linda," Ruth said. "She's a really good person who put a lot of herself into getting to know us. I think we're obligated to help her in any way we can."

There was a pause while we all contemplated the decision we had seemingly reached to ask Jean and her kids to live with us. I felt there was a happy excitement just ready to burst loose.

"Let's talk about space for a minute," Gary suggested. "Where would everybody fit?" I was really pleased by Gary's practical involvement in the house, even though he would be gone. It spoke to me of an interest and bonds which were more complex and durable than friendship alone, it spoke to me of community.

"I've been thinking about that, too," Leigh said seriously. "If the three kids could share Gary and Anne's room–it's probably big enough, and we could build partitions–that would open up Matt's room for Jean."

I was thinking about the logistics of that suggestion when Leigh continued, sounding even more thoughtful.

"But what's really on my mind," she said, "is that Dan and I have had separate rooms for most of the year, and next year he's going to be down at the hospital every day and a few nights a week, so that'll give me a lot of privacy. So I was thinking, Ruth, if he and I shared my room, you could have Dan's room. Would that be okay with you, Dan?"

"Sure," he said, laconically.

Ruth had not been expecting Leigh to make that sacrifice, it had never crossed her mind that Leigh would offer to give up a room of her own so that she might have one. It was a gesture both emblematic and real, and one which conveyed a sincerity on Leigh's part which moved Ruth to want to laugh

162

or to cry; she felt a swelling of affection for Leigh, a gratitude, which made her voice catch, when she said,

"You'll have to think about that. I really know how much you'd be giving up, and how much you're saying to me by making that offer."

The two women looked at each other levelly; both flushed. There was a celebratory tension in the room.

"You know once an offer like that is made seriously it can't be rescinded, Leigh," Anne said to her friend, wanting to concretize the moment. "Once Ruth gets a room of her own you can't really change your mind after a couple of months and ask for it back."

"I know," Leigh said simply.

"Maybe everybody should think about it some more," Gary advised. He turned to Dan. "There's something else I want to say. Dan, all these things concern you as much as anybody, but mostly you've just sat there smiling and it leaves me in the dark about where you're at."

Dan smiled and shrugged, and Gary stood up, took hold of him, and shook him vigorously by the shoulders.

"I don't know," Dan said. "I guess I've said whatever's on my mind."

So we had reached a decision, and along the way our accommodations to each other had begun to incline toward the future. Gary and Anne were leaving, and yet their involvement with the house seemed greater than Dan's, who was staying. A new family was moving in, and though Ruth and Leigh seemed to be jealous of Jean's friendship, they had also pledged more to each other than either had anticipated.

The next day we talked to Jean, and a few days later Linda came to visit and we told her of our decision. And then, just when it all seemed settled, Jean changed her mind and decided to live instead with a man who had been resisting her suggestions that he share her home. By the time that happened, Linda had helped to form another house. We were dreadfully let down, none of us more than Matt, and we began to look again.

*　　*　　*

It was still spring and there was much that was good in our lives. The backyard were sunbathing warm. Much time was spent outdoors. We often ate supper in the backyard at twilight, carrying out gigantic salads and jugs of wine or lemonade from the kitchen. It was time to transplant, and our vegetables went into the ground.

But there was a prospect nagging at Leigh's peace of mind. Across the Delaware River, in Camden, N.J., a federal Grand Jury was convened. Among the first witness es called were Leigh's brother and sister-in-law. He was summoned from the jail cell where he was serving time for attempting to destroy draft board records; she had been arrested at the same time, but acquitted. Now, both of them refused to answer the Grand Jury's questions about their friends, and the government asked a judge to grant them immunity from prosecution. This was, in fact, no more than the Nixon Justice Department's way of threatening them with prison terms: once they were granted immunity they could no longer claim their Fifth Amendment right against self-incrimination, and so were compelled to testify or be sentenced for contempt. They chose the latter, and were sent to prison. And Leigh, who was close to both of them and who had been active herself in anti-war work, began to think that she might soon be a prisoner of the state.

"I have this real fear that I'm going to be behind bars in a few months," she said at a house meeting. "I was just realizing that I feel a lot more together about it than I used to. I used to have all these fantasies that I'd be really alone, that Dan would get immediately involved with somebody else. And I would end up sitting there in that fucking jail and writing him these letters and not getting any response. And what's happened now is that that's still a fear I have, but I've got you people who I trust won't desert me. And so I don't have to put all that fantasized paranoia on Dan."

"Listen," said Chris, "if you go to jail I'll visit and bring chicken soup."

Slowing Down

We glided into and out of each moment toward one of those conjunctions which are tallied as the small change of fate; the Fourth of July, yes, Independence Day, was when Gary and Anne would leave.

* * *

The spring clean. Scrubbing the woodwork. M'god, it was *white*. And the floors, scrubbed and polished, they glowed with the darkness of seventy years' use. A shampoo for the carpets, foaming them sweet and clean. Yes, and the freezer's ice was melted away, an indoors thaw. Look! A clean window is a thing of joy, glistening with sunlight, thrown open to the fragrant freezes. When the sky was full of evening, the living room and dining room were streaked with light and shadow from the orange sun dipping behind the trees across the way. It looked fine, all of it. Like a home.

* * *

In May, Pete met Sara. It did not take long before he began to know that what was stirring in his mind and his heart had a force of some consequence. Spring melted into summer. "I ain't a youngster any more," he thought. He tried to be open to what life would bring, but he . . . wanted. Oh, god how he wanted, how we all wanted, want. What? lover? home? work? child?

*   *   *

Pete and Ruth were standing in the front hall at live o'clock in the evening during the first week of June when he took a step forward and put his arms around her. The hug lasted a long time during which Pete felt the satisfaction of having given Ruth something of value at last. Much which they had hoped for themselves was not yet theirs. They were not intimate, neither lovers nor confidants. Both had acknowledged in the privacy of their musings that they would take up what new responsibilities descended upon them when Gary and Anne flew away. After the wondrous tension relaxed, Pete laughed, a sound like a whinny, and said, "Chimps hug when they're afraid, and they're our closest precursors."

*   *   *

We had moved a set of battered old speakers into the yard and often, after dinner, I wandered out into the dusky summer evening to be alone on the white bench under the rhododendron and watch the stone-solid broad back of our house. An unused television aerial stood on the sloping roof, its electric awkwardness rising above the house, trailing wires. The lights were on in the living room, and somebody, I could not be sure who, was moving in there. Gussie nudged open the screen door out behind the kitchen with a thick, old shoulder, sniffed the air, and lumbered down the three short steps into the yard. It was a moment before she noticed me and trotted over to ask for a scratch. Across the width of the three small windows that were banked on the front landing Pete appeared, crossed, and descended out of sight. On the third floor a lamp was switched on in Gary and Anne's room, like a golden revelation. A bird called. The house was taking on its night appearance, shadows closing into darkness. I was restless. I stood and walked back toward the inside, bare feet brushed by cool, damp grass. Writing about our house was giving me a profound intellectual attachment to our life together: I felt at peace.

*　　*　　*

The men in the shiny black shoes and the gabardine suits knock on the door at seven in the morning. Leigh wakes with a start. While I turn over and readjust myself to the warm contours of my bed, thinking sleepily that they should go away, whoever they are, Leigh KNOWS. She slips on a light blue cotton nightgown and hurries down the wide blue-green carpeted steps. Sunlight falls in streaks on the hardwood floor of the front hall. She opens the top of the front door, leaving the bottom barred, and the man in the Permapress white shirt and the narrow gold and navy striped tie asks,

"Leigh Lawrence?"

She puts out her hand and takes the folded document, shuts the door, and opens it to read:

"You are hereby commanded to appear in the United States District Court for the District of New Jersey in the city of Camden on June 26 . . ."

*　　*　　*

Which summons did not, however, prevent her from going ahead with an excursion she had planned to take with Chris, Dan, and Joan–who had moved to Philadelphia and become a frequent visitor at the house. One night after dark arrived they stirred up a concoction of mescaline, LSD, and orange juice and took turns swallowing it. Dan soon loped out into the yard where it was wet and dripping and climbed the massive oak to his favorite perch in the cradle of a big bough about twenty-five feet above the ground.

Whoosh the rush tingled the other three in all their many funny bones there on the giggly green carpet when I appeared with a soft sweet wet purple plum and took a–juices drooled lusciously over the ripped purple skin, revealing the deep yellow pulp–bite.

"A plum," said the awestruck Leigh. "May I touch the plum?"

I handed it to her. They played with the plum before eating it, it had a mysterious novelty.

Soon Joan too disappeared into the backyard, where Leigh imagined she and Dan were fucking high in the bower, each of them swinging by a hand from the nearest limb while they invented the most graceful and satisfying positions known to man or monkey.

Later, all standing together around the garden, they watched the vegetables . . . grow! There before their very eyes! In the silver moon-washed wet.

But Dan, who came in and curled up his body with the rest in front of the warm, drying fire, was on a trip of his own. He felt the fierce female wills of Leigh and Joan pulling at him until the sensation was of being ripped slowly apart by his own desires and theirs. He left first to go to bed, while Joan and Leigh sat on the front steps as the sun rose and talked in a friendly way about the mysteries of the dark, sensual, receding night.

And Dan, who was a stranger to the thought that there were situations beyond his control or capabilities, Dan, who had–*he* would never say this, but it was his anchor always succeeded by doing what he could see needed to be done, Dan could no longer put off what he must do because the pain of many desires tore dreadfully at the secure center of his certainty. And so at a house meeting, our last as nine, he said to Leigh:

"I'm more torn apart than I can handle. The reality is that I only have enough energy for you. I love you."

And Leigh took a quick, startled look at that profession of constancy and attachment, palpable there between them, glanced, and then darted for safety. She equivocated.

But like a brick wall she found us blocking her retreat.

"Look," we said in the collective voice of the house. "*This* is what you've been asking Dan to give you for a whole year now and more. Well, now that you've got it you can't run away."

*   *   *

The house meeting continued. Yakity yak yak yak. And Anne drew deeper and deeper into the big soft green chair until she was no more than a little ball of pink flesh and blond hair in the furthest corner, hardly noticeable. And just before she was about to disappear altogether I called out,

"Hello, Anne."

She looked at me across the room and began to grow a bit, but not much.

"How are you over there?" I yahooed.

But I knew how she was. So I went over and climbed up beside her because there was a lot of room in that great big chair. Room enough for nine of us, as it quickly turned out.

Tuesday, June 12, the sun disappeared behind a bank of heavy gray rain clouds and nobody saw it again for two weeks. It began to drizzle and then to rain and for all those days the air was heavy and wet. The Schuylkill River flooded its banks and washed out the river drives. Ruth said it restored her respect for the industry-blighted, man assaulted Schuylkill–it was a river after all, with a river's power to do damage. On the eleventh day the temperatures dropped twenty degrees and even that was a relief. We in the urban east have no weather much of the year, just skies which shift between dim gray and dim blue, and changes in temperature. So the torrential rain, because it was weather at last, was a treat, no matter how perverse. By the end of the first week people on the buses stopped telling each other, "Well, it's good for the farmers," because they were no longer themselves indifferent to the weather. It had affected them, the mood of the entire city was gripped by the clouds, was sodden and anxious.

At breakfast on the twelfth day Pete talked about the orgiastic sun worship of the ancient Scandinavians at the end of the lightless winter. He was sitting in the gloomy kitchen eating sunflower seeds, wheatsils, cashews, raisins, dried apricots, and wheat germ out of a white ceramic bowl half filled with cold milk, and sipping from a cup of coffee.

169

The vegetable garden grew tropic. Our marijuana plants shot up taller than me. I began to imagine that the day the weather broke and the sun reappeared the whole city would steam and grow wild, the vegetation would sprout spontaneously out of the long dormant earth and burrow its way up through the concrete and asphalt and tarmac shattering the downtown office buildings and rendering the city nibble.

Our life slowed way down as we strained against the certain departure of days. We made our pace slow and easy as we could. Dan was swallowed up by the hospital, and we prepared to accompany Leigh to the Grand Jury. We held tight to ourselves and to each other under those goddamn gray skies and waited for the time to unravel its surprises. Actually, we were remarkably confident about ourselves and our strength. Not happy, precisely, but alive to the possibilities of each moment.

September 26, 1973

Epilogue

Years ago an old friend told me he suspected that I brought people together and observed them so that I could write about them, that I was constructing a book out of my life, or my life out of an idea for a book. Evidently he was right.

With only seven of us living together during the second year the house seemed roomier, slower-paced, less crowd ed with people and their demands and activities. By autumn the Grand Jury no longer seemed to be interested in Leigh, although it was many months before we were certain that she would not be forced to testify. She changed her mind a number of times, but in the end moved with us to San Francisco. Dan took off in a different direction: when his internship was completed he bought a house not far from where he grew up and began to practice. For the time being, he's a small-town doc. Chris has moved to the Bay Area, but is living in another house. For Pete, this last year has been painful and tumultuous–he still hasn't decided whether or not to move to San Francisco. Linda and her daughter Bea continued to be friendly with us, and now they're living in our new house, a rambling Victorian affair with two-dozen rooms. There are four children in the house, including Anne and Gary's new son and Ruth's and my baby daughter.

*   *   *

On Cliveden street I learned how necessary it was to let the people in the house be evasive at times, to let them hold back. We all needed space in which to be ourselves, realms in which we were unanswerable. But there was also a necessity for candor. Without it, there was a daily seepage of good feelings into the gunk hole of annoyance, injustice collecting and ill-ease.

Writing this book put into a public dimension my effort to strike a balance between giving the other people in the house as wide a berth as each of them required, while also trying to be forthright with them. No book tells all, but I write in order to tell as much as I can of what I know. When I compromise, I left with a character deficiency, as surely as a bread and water diet would leave me with a vitamin deficiency. But the kind of candor wanted by one's friends is far less rigorous than what is demanded by trying to write the truth of what one thinks. By changing the names of the people in the house I hoped to conceal their identities–but only from strangers. I wrote with the actual people and their vulnerabilities always in mind, and so I held back, and suffered whatever damage to my character such a withholding causes. But, however unwittingly, I also reflected the actuality of what *I* was like in the house.

*　　*　　*

One day during the second year I was in my room writing about Leigh and Ruth and some of the problems they were having the year before. Leaving them to wait for me in my typewriter, I went down to the kitchen to make a cup of tea. And there, perched on the red stool, was the real Leigh, with no reason to expect that I would be anything but friendly. How could she possibly know that I was angry at her re-created self for what she had just-that-moment-a-year-before said to Ruth? But to have explained to her, to have relocated myself in the complications of the then and–there of the kitchen, would have meant relinquishing my mind–grip on the Leigh waiting for me upstairs in my typewriter. I was curt, and left the kitchen as soon as I could.

Having to make choices of that kind, taken together with the kind of considerate, emotive, empathetic behavior valued in the house makes me think that writing while living communally is a considerable risk. I wonder if in order to write honestly and fully I won't have to be more self absorbed than is possible in a commune like ours. And I worry that I gain the way I live at the expense of my work, that collectivity leads to self-censorship–and self censorship, after all, is fatal for a writer. But where else can I work if not in the swarm of my own life? At the moment, whether it's because I'm too cowardly to strike out on my own or because I'm ambitious beyond all reason, I want a good life and good work, both.

And so I continue to bump and jostle on down the line, wondering all the while how I've ended up on the rush hour bus of our lives together. Somewhere along the way I had decided that it wasn't necessary to be lonely everywhere just because at the core I would always be alone. I was ready to chance being awkward or foolish or mistaken because small risks were bringing me small satisfactions. So I climbed aboard by taking a step toward the unknown, and then another, and another, and another . . .

174

Palo Alto, California
January, 2013

Catching Up: What Happened Next and Where We Are Now

With Chris, Dan and Pete no longer living with us, plus the addition of three new communards – Linda and her daughter Bea, and Hal, a doctor who was a friend of Gary and Anne – the dynamic changed in the new house on Fair Oaks street in San Francisco. Even forty years later I don't know how to describe the change except to say that the mix of new people with the rest of us who had been there from the beginning never took on the old shoe comfort and warmth we eventually shared on Cliveden Street. There was still a wheel of weekly housekeeping chores on the fridge, we still pooled our cars and half our incomes, we continued to hold house meetings every week but there were lots of new relationships and the old timers, myself included, no longer seemed to care as much about working everything through and giving everybody his or her turn at the center of attention. There were also two new infants: Gary and Anne's son Hyim, and Ruth and my daughter Bessie. Their parents' attention and involvement naturally was with their newborns. And, in addition, both marriages were faltering.

In July, 1973, we bought three contiguous Victorians on a pleasant side street in a sunny part of town for $72,000. Gary and Anne put down $5,000 as did the newcomer Hal; one partner couldn't afford to contribute; Ruth and I kicked in $375, all we had left from my book advance. Because we did not intend to ever sell and also because we were egalitarian communalists we agreed that if we ever reached the unlikely decision to sell the houses all profits would be divided equally among us. We didn't draw up a contract. The agreement was casually arrived at. We imagined our future would be an ever improving present.

The actual future arrived soon enough. Only a year after we moved to San Francisco we agreed – with a good deal of awkward tension – to disband the commune and to decide who would live in each of the three row houses and who would leave. Our time together ended for the same kinds of reasons so many marriages collapse: we were tired of trying so hard, and of each other; we wanted to see what it would be like on our own; what had been surprising or exciting became predictable and annoying; we hoped for fresh starts, new directions. The time for communal living had come and its time had gone. We talked a lot about honesty but were not especially straight forward. In the end it was Hal, the newcomer and largest investor, who didn't get a place. He was, understandably I see now, furious.

The two married couples continued to raise our young kids as next door neighbors and as if they were step-siblings. But by 1977 Gary and Anne had split up and Ruth and I were on the verge of separating. All the partners in the Fair Oaks property – this included Pete who had invested in the new property while continuing to live in Philadelphia - agreed the time had come to sell the houses. Sheepish though the idea made us, a reasonable profit no longer seemed criminal. A real estate agent told us we could get $250,000. A quarter of a million dollars! For the first time in two years we all sat down together to talk things over. Hal, who had in his view already been screwed once, came with a lawyer. The rest of us recoiled, feeling that our principles were being betrayed. But Hal felt that he had been done wrong, that the trust underlying our communal understandings no longer existed or mattered. Once our common vision had been our basis of cooperation but now what bound us was the common ownership of a valuable property. The meeting ended in rancor. All the rest of us hired our own lawyer. Hal's lawyer and ours began to exchange letterheads, billing us whenever they did. And with every month that passed the value of the houses increased. We watched ourselves riding the wave of a real estate boom with a mixture of irony and awe.

Finally, a few weeks before the end of 1979, I walked into a title company and picked up one of those discreet manila envelopes with a cellophane window. The check inside was for twice as much money as I had ever earned in a year; all the other communards received similar checks. Hal received more than anybody else but not as much as he had sought. The commune that we had created almost a decade earlier in order to live outside the constraints of consumer capitalism was kaput, and we were all better off than we had ever been. What can I say?

Looking back now, nearly forty years later, certain things seem apparent. It seems naïve now to have believed that a jerry-built communal household, formed in response to a social and political order that we abhorred because it had brought us the war in Vietnam, inequality and racism – and *that* was just the beginning of our grievances - would itself survive the rapacious appetites of chew-'em-up and spit -'em-out capitalism. It was a time when our hopes and good intentions masqueraded as plans, when it seemed possible to overcome one's unavoidable aloneness by an act of collective will. I don't regret a moment of it. The ties I still feel to my boon companions are not dissimilar to family ties: I am close to some of the communards to this day; I've lost track of others; and still others I seldom if ever see or talk to. But I am forever bound to all of them in memory and because we built something together that sustained us for awhile and made us feel we were responding to the particular challenges of our time.

Simply because the commune did not prove durable doesn't mean it didn't succeed. As part of preparing this new edition I sent emails to my old compatriots and fellow travelers asking them two questions. The first was how they wanted to be described now in 2013, and the second was whether they objected to my publishing their real names.

None of us knew how to contact Chris; he had disappeared from our lives many years ago. "Gary" – Dr. Bob Ross – was murdered by a crazy old man with an imagined grudge against him. Bob was 39-years old, the founding medical director of the Caleb G. Clark Potrero Hill Health Center in San Francisco, serving the destitute and desperate residents of one of the city's nastiest housing projects.

His wife "Anne" – Arlene Shmaeff – is an artist, an educator, "a partner to my wonderful husband, a mother and grandmother," she wrote. "I am very involved in my work as an educator and continue to see my work in the context of a greater political vision. I can definitely trace the planting of the seeds of that vision to my experience of being part of the commune and interacting with the amazing people I lived with."

What shone through the responses was how enriched most of us felt by our years together on Cliveden Street and Fair Oaks Street, and the warmth of our affections.

"Leigh" – Gale Bataille – founded and directed a residential program for young adults in the Bay Area and eventually became a county mental health director in three different counties. Now retired, she continues to work as a consultant. "I have had two wonderful marriages [her first husband died in 1993]," she wrote, "and rich and sometimes complicated relationships with children and grandchildren through extended families that were foreshadowed by that intentional family of the 1970's. One of my [communal] housemates and several extended community members remain among my closest friends."

"Dan" – Dr. Ron Hess – wrote: "My 28 year old daughter married a very nice guy from Buenos Aires...she is doing a Ph.D. in environmental and earth science...my 24-year old son graduated from Stanford and is a product manager at a high tech company. We're still in Los Altos and I'm still practicing neurology. In my spare time I hike and ride my bike up into the hills. Terese and I have a great backyard garden complete with bee hive and chickens. I'm still playing mandolin, and am taking flying lessons so I can get up to our place in Mendocino more easily."

"Pete" – he wants only his first name, Steve, to be used – came to California to be a Research Associate at U.C. Berkeley several years after the rest of us arrived in California, and by then he was married. He is the father of two daughters and the founder of a successful business. A few years ago his older daughter took over the business. "Not surprisingly," he wrote, "she is doing a much better job of it than I ever did....I have often thought through these years that my transition to the latter stage of my life would not have been possible if I had not lived *Living Together.* For this I am and will be always grateful to the people depicted in this book for putting up with me and providing me with some needed lessons in living life!"

My ex-wife "Ruth" – Berne Weiss – wrote: "I am an undeterred idealist who went to see the Velvet Revolution up close and ended up living in Budapest, which is too far from my three grandchildren. I am a member of the Budapest Quaker Meeting, and I have a private therapy practice for people who dream in English. I am currently working on a project imagining the world without war, seeing as how humans had to imagine flying before they could pull it off."

Our son "Matt" – Josh Weiss – lives in Denver, Colorado, with his wife Margaret and his children Mason and Audrey. "I would like to say," he wrote, "that I found my own way to rebel against my upbringing by joining the mainstream overseeing rules and regulations in the financial services industry." I suppose I have only myself to blame for having raised such a sharp-witted, clear-sighted son.

Bob Ross and Arlene Shmaeff's son, Hyim, is a musician with an international career, and is a campaigner for world peace and understanding. He shares with his late father his musicality and his passion for justice. Berne's and my daughter Bess is the mother of a seven-year old son, and a successful editor and publishing executive. She and Hyim – forty years after they were born into our commune and raised side by side for the first years of their lives – consider themselves to be brother and sister.

180

Mike Weiss is the Edgar Award-winning author of *Double Play: The Hidden Passions Behind the Double Assassination of George Moscone and Harvey Milk*. In addition to writing for the San Francisco Chronicle, his work has appeared in Rolling Stone, Esquire, Mother Jones, The Guardian, and many other publications. He is also the author of the acclaimed Ben Henry series of mystery novels and the non-fiction book *A Very Good Year: The Journey of a California Wine from Vine to Table*.

Printed in Great Britain
by Amazon.co.uk, Ltd.,
Marston Gate.